The French Royal Wardrobe

THE HÔTEL DE LA MARINE RESTORED

Flammarion

ÉDITIONS DU PATRIMOINE
CENTRE DES MUSÉES
MONUMENTS NATIONAUX

FLAMMARION

Executive Editor
Suzanne Tise-Isoré
Style & Design Collection

Editorial Adviser
Karine Huguenaud

Editorial Coordination
Lara Lo Calzo

Editorial Assistant
Virginie Picat

Graphic Design
Bernard Lagacé

Translation from the French
Deke Dusinberre

Copy editing and Proofreading
Lindsay Porter

Production
Corine Trovarelli

Color Separation
Les Artisans du Regard, Paris

Printed in Italy by Verona Libri

CENTER FOR NATIONAL MONUMENTS

President
Philippe Bélaval

Executive Director
Delphine Samsoen

CONSERVATION OF MONUMENTS
AND COLLECTIONS
Director
Delphine Christophe

CULTURAL AND PUBLIC DEVELOPMENT
Director
Edward de Lumley

Department of Documentary Resources
Department Manager
Laurent Bergeot

Manager, Picture Department
Anne Lesage

Librarian, Picture Department
Blanche Legendre

Photographer, Picture Department
Benjamin Gavaudo

HÔTEL DE LA MARINE
Administrator
Jocelyn Bouraly

And all the team at the Hôtel
de la Marine

ÉDITIONS DU PATRIMOINE
Editorial Director
Antoine Gründ

hôtel de
la marine

© Flammarion S.A., Paris, 2021
© Éditons du Patrimoine,
Centre des monuments nationaux,
Paris, 2021
www.monuments-nationaux.fr

Simultaneously published in French as
*Le Garde-Meuble de la Couronne,
Le temps retrouvé à l'Hôtel de la Marine.*
© Flammarion S.A., Paris, 2021

English language edition
© Flammarion S.A., Paris, 2021

Flammarion S.A.
87, quai Panhard-et-Levassor
75647 Paris cedex 13
editions.flammarion.com
@styleanddesignflammarion

21 22 23 3 2 1
ISBN: 978-2-08-026132-8
Legal Deposit: 10/2021

ENDPAPERS Details of a silk lampas fabric with scrolling foliage, seahorses, and beribboned dogs. The silk wall-linings in Marc Antoine Thierry de Ville-d'Avray's bedroom were rewoven by the Tassinari & Chatel firm, based on eighteenth-century archives.

FACING PAGE In the large antechamber, a wall fountain of Carrara marble (c. 1740) is topped by a gilded sculpture of a child playing with a swan, set against a sky-blue background.

PAGES 4–5 Pierre Antoine Demachy (1723–1807), *Fanciful View of the Royal Wardrobe,* oil on canvas, 1792 (Musée du Louvre, Paris).

PAGES 6–7 Jacques Guiaud (1810–1876), *The Return of Napoleon's Ashes to Paris, December 15, 1840* (detail), oil on canvas, 1841 (Châteaux de Versailles et de Trianon, Versailles). The procession moved through Place de la Concorde, where the obelisk given to France by the viceroy of Egypt, Mehmet Ali, was erected in 1836.

PAGES 8–9 Carlo Bossoli (1815–1884), *Place de la Concorde,* pen and ink, watercolor, gouache, 1853 (private collection).

The French Royal Wardrobe

THE HÔTEL DE LA MARINE RESTORED

text Jérôme Hanover and Gabriel Bauret

photography Ambroise Tézenas

Contents

PAGE 10 An employee of the Department of the Navy watching a crowd gathering on Place de la Concorde; the photo is dated October 22, 1898 (Sammlung Archiv für Kunst und Geschichte, Berlin).

PAGE 11 The covered passage beneath the arcade of the Hôtel de la Marine on Place de la Concorde; the photo is dated July 1965.

PAGES 12–13 Rue Royale and the Church of La Madeleine seen from Place de la Concorde; photo c. 1900.

PAGES 14–15 Awards ceremony in the main courtyard of the Department of the Navy; photo dated March 15, 1927, Rols News Agency (Bibliothèque Nationale de France, Paris).

PAGES 16–17 Place de la Concorde on a rainy night, 1935.

PAGES 18–19 The façade of the Hôtel de la Marine on Place de la Concorde. The central colonnade is flanked by two corner pavilions crowned by triangular pediments with sculpted groups, *Royal Magnificence* (left, by Michel-Ange Slodtz) and *Public Happiness* (right, by Guillaume Coustou the Younger).

PAGES 20–21 A view of Place de la Concorde from the loggia of the Hôtel de la Marine.

FACING PAGE A view of the ground-level arcade for pedestrians and, above, the colonnade of the Hôtel de la Marine.

Foreword

The extensive work on the Hôtel de la Marine, led by the Center for National Monuments (*Centre des Monuments Nationaux*) from 2017 to 2021, was a complex operation that revealed all the talents of the teams brought together for this project.

What did it actually entail? First of all, it involved the restoration of glamorous premises built late in the ancien régime by one of France's finest architects, Ange Jacques Gabriel. Although occupied by the Department of the Navy (*Marine*) for 226 years, the nature of these premises was never irrevocably altered, hence they are now considered by specialists to be an authentic model of eighteenth-century building skills.

Next, adaptations were required in order to open this remarkable building to the wider public for the first time in its long history. The infrastructure needed to be modernized, security facilities had to be updated, and the requirements of those who came to work in or visit the building had to be addressed. Space had to be found for a café, restaurant, offices, and all the services needed to welcome the hundreds of thousands of people who will come to the Hôtel de la Marine in the future for one reason or another.

Finally, the interior decoration and atmosphere of the highly delicate heritage rooms had to be recreated. The result is one of the most refined urban residences of the Enlightenment era, evoking a now rare example of French lifestyle and savoir-faire.

This long-term restoration project, an outstanding achievement that owes much to the support of numerous public and private lenders, involved almost every field of the arts and crafts. It was closely followed by Ambroise Tézenas, whose photographs offer readers rare insight into a human as well as a cultural saga.

These pictures constitute a lasting record. Artworks in themselves, they will become part of the history of the building, enabling future generations to experience the rebirth of a remarkable example of French heritage.

PHILIPPE BÉLAVAL
President of the Centre des Monuments Nationaux

FACING PAGE The entrance to the large study of the intendant-general of the Royal Wardrobe, Marc Antoine Thierry de Ville-d'Avray.

The Royal Wardrobe, High and Low

JÉRÔME HANOVER

VUE DU GARDE MEUBLE DE LA
COURONNE

Testard del.

Roger sculp.

A Paris, chez les Campions freres, rue S.ᵗ Jacques, à la Ville de Rouen.

Avec Priv. du Roi.

France's Royal Warehouse

More or less all royal households in Europe had a department like the Royal Wardrobe (*Garde-Meuble de la Couronne*), in one form or another. These administrative departments were part of the machinery of government, somewhat cold and distant. Often their historic names now mean little to people. In eighteenth-century England, the Office of the Great Wardrobe was not just a storehouse for the king's ceremonial robes and the supplier of cloths and hangings for a full range of state occasions, it also commissioned all kinds of hard furnishings and decorative furniture for royal residences, as did its French counterpart.

In France, the Garde-Meuble is remembered for the spectacular theft of the crown jewels during the French Revolution, which continues to instill a kind of paradoxical nostalgia in the collective unconscious. France's Royal Wardrobe furthermore benefited from King Louis XV's determination to transform one of his household offices into a true political tool. By installing the Wardrobe in an architectural masterpiece on a square named after himself, Louis was sending a message to the whole world, demonstrating the grandeur of the French state and the genius of French arts. Today this would be called "soft power." Now open to the public, these premises raise a former royal warehouse to the status of a leading museum of decorative arts.

Because, quite prosaically, a warehouse is what it was: the Wardrobe is what was called at the time a "magazine"—from the Arabic *maḥazin* (مخازن), the plural of "storehouse." The Royal Wardrobe was in charge of commissioning, maintaining, and storing royal furnishings, that is to say the crown's moveable goods, as opposed to the crown's immoveable "real estate" in the form of royal residences. Movables included the hard furnishings we call "furniture" today, as well as soft furnishings such as gold-brocade fabrics, draperies, tapestries, and also practical items such as silverware, bronzes, valuable arms and armor, and even the crown jewels. All these extremely costly "moveables" had to be stored somewhere when not in use—for example, the coronation canopy, by definition, was used just once per reign. And royal residences were only fully furnished when the king was actually living there; the more fragile furnishings would be removed between stays.

France's royal warehouse thus acquired its noble title when it moved into a building designed by architect Ange Jacques Gabriel on a square—now called Place de la Concorde—that remains one of the largest in Paris. The Wardrobe completely occupied the building for a mere fifteen years. It was the subsequent tenant, the Department of the Navy (*Marine*), which occupied the premises for the next two hundred years and gave the building its current name: Hôtel de la Marine.

Yet these were the premises that forged the legend of France's Royal Wardrobe. And, miraculously preserved, they perpetuate that legend today. This building is an accumulation of countless histories—political, artistic, investigative, judicial. When the Navy left the building to join the other armed forces, it created a breach into which history immediately leaped: the spirit of the historic Royal Wardrobe was just waiting to re-occupy the setting in which it rose to glory. The museum now installed in the intendant-general's apartment, thanks to the expertise contributed by Joseph Achkar and Michel Charrière, brings the eighteenth century—the heyday of France's Royal Wardrobe—back to life.

29

PAGE 27 Detail of the colonnade of the loggia of the Hôtel de la Marine.
FACING PAGE Roger Barthélemy, (1770–1841), after Jean Testard, *View of the Royal Wardrobe,* print published in *Vues Pittoresques des Principaux Edifices de Paris,* 1787–1792 (Bibliothèque Nationale de France, Paris).

ABOVE Alexis Nicolas Pérignon
(1726–1782), *View of Place Louis XV
Prior to Construction of the Bridge*,
pen and India ink, watercolor,
gouache, (Bibliothèque Nationale
de France, Paris).

The Ministry of High Style

The history of the Royal Wardrobe, like the building that housed it, began long before the two merged. The department was already one hundred and seventy years old when it left the Hôtel des Ambassadeurs Extraordinaires (today's Élysée Palace) to move to Place Louis XV (now Place de la Concorde). The Wardrobe was established in 1604 to coordinate King Henri IV's major refurbishing of châteaus in Fontainebleau, Saint-Germain-en-Laye, and elsewhere, as well as to centralize scattered departments of the royal household. At the time, the Wardrobe dealt mainly with soft furnishings, because Henri was not a great fan of "design," so to speak. Since the Wardrobe had to store old furnishings as well as to commission new ones, it was mathematically destined to grow over time. The curve of growth was proportional to the interest a given king took in the arts, in symbols of the crown's magnificence, and in the development of his estates. Unsurprisingly, the prize goes to Louis XIV, who "launched a policy of prestige that included the lifestyle of the royal family and the entire court, which he intended to be magnificent. The king first modernized the interior decoration of existing palaces such as the Louvre, the Tuileries, and Saint-Germain-en-Laye, then he enlarged Versailles and built Marly and Trianon.... To monitor the ever-expanding, increasingly varied and costly furnishings, a household administration more rigorous than those of previous reigns was required."[1] From that period date the earliest surviving inventories. Prior to then, "nothing was in order," according to Gaspard Moïse de Fontanieu, intendant-general of the Royal Wardrobe from 1719 to 1767.[2] Although some damaged or no-longer-fashionable items were sold or destroyed—metals were melted down, and fabrics were burned in order to recover the gold thread—the main thrust was clearly growth. Apart from the importance of the department itself, the office of intendant-general was highly glamorous because the holder "took his orders directly from the king and members of the royal family," which was not true of any other departmental director within the royal household.[3]

The role of the intendant-general of the Royal Wardrobe was complementary to the task of the director of the Office of Royal Works (*Bâtiments du Roi*). Given their influence over the king, these two men defined "the French style" and ensured the development of a lifestyle specific to each period—one was in charge of content (furnishings), the other of container (buildings). Obviously, all decisions remained with the king, and the interest shown by Louis XIV and Louis XV in architecture and style called for a highly sound—or at least, clear—sense of taste. But through the choice of artists he introduced to the king, and the stylistic arguments he employed, the intendant-general could encourage, prompt, and guide artistic developments of his day, at the very least nudging them, at best directing them. Pierre Élisabeth de Fontanieu, the first intendant-general to move into Gabriel's new building under Louis XV, could probably boast that he introduced work by cabinetmaker Jean Henri Riesener into the royal collection, thereby paving the way for what would become the very expression of the Louis-XVI style. The mechanism is exactly the same today—opinion makers drive changes in fashion. Salon gatherings were the social media of the day, with Marie-Antoinette the star influencer. Style, as defined by the items commissioned on behalf of the Royal Wardrobe, radiated from the upper

1. Stéphane Castelluccio, *Le Garde-Meuble de la Couronne et ses intendants, du XVIe au XVIIIe siècle* (Paris: Éditions du Comité des Travaux Historiques et Scientifiques, 2004), p. 16.
2. Ibid., p. 15.
3. Ibid., p. 17.

33

ABOVE Simon Charles Miger
(1736–1820), after Charles Nicolas
Cochin the Younger (1715–1790),
*Pierre Élisabeth de Fontanieu,
Intendant-General of the Royal
Wardrobe*, print, 1775 (Bibliothèque
Nationale de France, Paris).

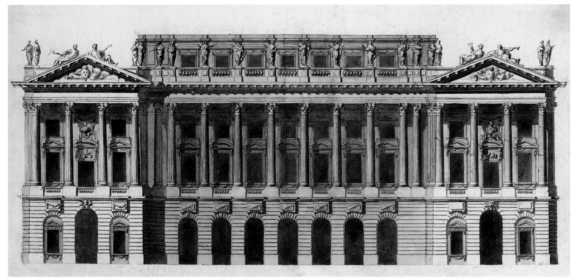

spheres of Versailles and other royal residences, creating envy in the mansions of wealthy tax farmers and filtering down to the bourgeois interiors of leading Paris worthies.

The Wardrobe became even more glamorous when Louis XV decided to move it to new premises on the square named after himself. When housed in the Hôtel du Petit-Bourbon, the Wardrobe had occupied a place tarred with infamy, since the townhouse had been confiscated from the Connétable de Bourbon when he betrayed King François I. The Hôtel du Petit-Bourbon was later razed to make way for the Louvre's new colonnade, and the Wardrobe, in search of other premises, was lodged in the Hôtel de Conti, which was not really designed for such use. But that was just a temporary move, for the city of Paris intended to erect its future town hall there; ultimately, the Mint was built on that site, and when work began, the Royal Wardrobe was obliged to move to the Hôtel des Ambassadeurs Extraordinaires, in premises ill-suited to its activities. At that same moment, however, the façades of the buildings on Place Louis XV were nearing completion, so "for the first time in a hundred years there arose the idea of housing the Wardrobe in a building adapted to its role. A makeshift arrangement was no longer good enough."[4] It is easy to imagine the excitement of the intendant-general as he moved in, even before work was completed,

4. Ibid., p. 109.
5. Ibid., p. 113.
6. Jacques Antoine Dulaure (1755–1835), a French historian and politician, was roughly thirty years old at the time.
7. Stéphane Castelluccio, "Le Garde-Meuble de la Couronne, 1770-1798," in *L'Hôtel de la Marine,* ed. Alexandre Gady, (Paris: Nicolas Chaudun, 2011).
8. Description from various archives quoted by Castelluccio, *Le Garde-Meuble de la Couronne et ses intendants,* p. 83.

ABOVE, TOP Anonymous, *Proposed Façade for the Royal Wardrobe on Place de la Concorde*, pen and ink, c. 1755 (Musée Carnavalet, Paris).
ABOVE, BOTTOM Attributed to Ange Jacques Gabriel (1698–1782), *Proposal for the Wardrobe,* pen and ink, undated (Musée Carnavalet, Paris).

some two years before the entire department could join him. Everything about the new premises made sense. "For obvious practical reasons, [architect Gabriel] allocated the ground floor to the kitchens, storehouses, and workshops. He placed the apartments and showrooms on the piano nobile facing the square and the side streets of Rue Saint-Florentin and Rue Royale; those rooms thus had the finest view, with the lively square below, and the river and Palais-Bourbon in the distance. The storerooms gave onto the inner courtyards."[5]

For the first time, the royal collection was open to the public, free of charge, one Tuesday per month, from April to November. The Royal Wardrobe became the first museum of decorative arts in Paris. "According to Dulaure,[6] it 'constituted one of the foremost curiosities in Paris for foreigners,' and it was probably also appreciated by art lovers from the provinces and Paris itself."[7] The goal was likely dual-purpose: on one hand, it would help to establish the fame and influence of French decorative arts (during that same period, the Marquis de Marigny, director of the Royal Works, suggested to the king that the Louvre be opened as a pendant museum for the fine arts, displaying the crown's collection of paintings); on the other hand, it would symbolize royal power and the permanency of the monarchy in a display that would strike every visitor. But it was also a doubled-edged sword. The costly lifestyle of the intendant-general—who lived in his official apartment like the king at Versailles— made an unfortunate impression during the French Revolution; the last intendant-general to serve under Louis XVI, Marc Antoine Thierry de Ville-d'Avray, was slaughtered in 1792, receiving "many blows of the sword to his head," "a pike thrust into his body," and "a burning torch in his mouth to silence him."[8] *O tempora, o mores*—what times, what customs!

Let us not get ahead of the story, however.

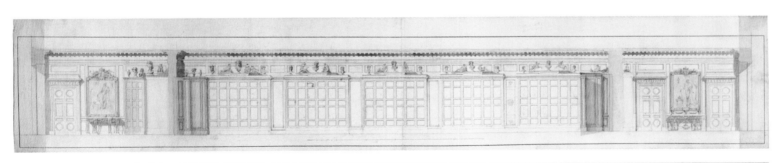

ABOVE Jean Démosthène Dugourc (1749–1825), *Cross-Section of the Gallery of Large Furnishings* and *The Gallery of Antiques in the Royal Wardrobe: Elevation of the South Wall with Sculptures Set into the Facing or Placed on Console Tables*, 1778 (Musée Carnavalet, Paris).

Great Utopian Plans

There were one hundred and fifty proposals for creating a new square in Paris to honor Louis XV, nicknamed "Louis the Well-Beloved," who had just brought peace to Europe by signing the Treaty of Aix-la-Chapelle.[9] The idea of installing the Royal Wardrobe there had not yet arisen. One hundred and fifty is not a figure of speech for "many"—roughly two-thirds of them have survived in one form or another. The enthusiasm generated by the project was truly phenomenal. "It is unbelievable how many masterpieces were produced by the rivalry and desire to outdo one another in this competition designed to celebrate our august Monarch," smugly commented Pierre Patte, an architect, theorist, and encyclopedist, in 1765.[10]

Architect Jacques Germain Soufflot proposed filling in the narrow stretch of the Seine between Île Saint-Louis and Île du Palais to form a square with a statue in the middle, flanked by the river to north and south. The east would be lined by private residences, while a bishop's palace would occupy the west side, near Notre-Dame. Germain Boffrand, meanwhile, designed a row of three squares running through the Halles marketplace, among "sellers of bread, vegetables, seafood, fresh-water fish … [and] clothiers, drapers, ironmongers, and merchants of every kind."[11] The idea was that the king would be enshrined among his people as a testimony to the prosperity he brought them—like Trajan with his imperial statue in the middle of the marketplace of ancient Rome. The site suggested by both Laurent Destouches and Jean-Michel Chevotet[12] was directly opposite the Louvre colonnade, already viewed as the crowning achievement of French classicism despite having been so decried when it was built eighty years earlier. Destouches's proposal was aligned with the portal of the existing Church of Saint-Germain l'Auxerrois, while Chevotet had no qualms about demolishing the entire neighborhood, church included (which he suggested rebuilding further back, opposite the Pont Neuf). Martin Goupy[13] favored the Left Bank (as did many others, in order to avoid the costly center of Paris), on the corners of Rue de Belle-Chasse and Rue de Bourbon (today Bellechasse and Lille), where he would erect buildings for four ministries: War, Clergy, Foreign Affairs—and Navy. The statue of Louis XV in the middle of the square would thereby face the one of Louis XIV (his great-grandfather) erected in Place Vendôme all the way across the Seine, across the Tuileries, across waves of rooftops, simultaneously creating an alignment of Rue de Bellechasse and Rue de Castiglione (which did not yet exist) on opposite sides of the central alley of the Tuileries Gardens laid out by André Le Nôtre.

If the proposals for a square to honor Louis XV were so different from one another, scattered all across town; if the symbolism they conveyed varied so greatly (whether religious, governmental, or commercial, whether evoking antiquity or recent dynasty); if so little account was taken of feasibility in terms of cost and property acquisition (government expropriation only became legal in France in 1810, and Louis XIV himself had to condition his Louvre construction projects on the willingness of nearby owners to sell to him); if, finally, the proposals seem to follow no rationale or need to develop the city, that is because the object of the competition wasn't "urbanistic." Above all, the future royal square was supposed to provide a setting for the bronze equestrian statue of Louis the Well-Beloved that the city of Paris wished to erect "as a mark of the zeal, love, and gratitude of his peoples."[14]

9. Alexandre Gady, "De la place Louis XV à la Concorde, vie et mort d'un espace royal," in *L'Hôtel de la Marine*.
10. Pierre Patte, *Monumens érigés en France à la gloire de Louis XV* (Paris: Chez l'Auteur, Desaint et Saillant, 1765), p. 120.
11. Ibid., p. 195.
12. Spelled Chevautet at the time.
13. Spelled Goupi at the time.
14. Patte, *Monumens érigés*, p. 120.

ABOVE Alexandre Roslin (1718–1793),
*Portrait of Marc Antoine Thierry
de Ville-d'Avray, Intendant-General
of the Wardrobe, 1732–1792,* oil on
canvas, 1790 (Châteaux de Versailles
et de Trianon, Versailles).

ABOVE *View of Place Louis XV
From the Saint-Honoré Gate in Paris,*
colored print, 1763 (Bibliothèque
Nationale de France, Paris).

In the Beginning was the Statue

And the statue was of the king; and the statue *was* king. Sculptor Edme Bouchardon was commissioned to make it. In 1748 Bouchardon was at the height of his fame—he had won the Prix de Rome twenty-five years earlier, was then fifty years old, taught at the Academy, and had earned royal accreditation. He was a blue-chip artist. "H[is] M[ajesty] having obligingly deferred to the enthusiasm of his subjects,"[15] the city of Paris ordered the statue from Bouchardon even as the director of the Office of Works (Charles François Paul Le Normant de Tournehem) launched the contest to design a square that would provide a worthy setting, on a level equal to the statue and to the king himself.

The king of bronze, in fact, was over twelve feet high, sitting on a horse almost fifteen feet high plus a base. In all, "thirty-three feet high from the ground to the top," according to a description by the artist himself, quoted by Alphonse Roserot.[16] It was colossal in terms of a human scale, perhaps, but perfectly proportioned to the designs by Soufflot, Boffrand, Destouches, and Goupy (and maybe even to the one by Chevotet). Yet the site ultimately chosen for the square was to the west of the Tuileries Gardens, at that time on the edge of Paris. When plopped down in the middle of a huge, twenty-acre esplanade open on three sides, the great king must have looked fairly insignificant.

Indeed, by the time the statue was unveiled, Louis no longer enjoyed high standing in the hearts of the French. More than thirteen years had passed between the day Bouchardon was awarded the commission on October 23, 1749, and the day the statue was unveiled on February 23, 1763.

15. Ibid., p. 117.
16. Alphonse Roserot, *Edme Bouchardon* (Paris: Librarie Central des Beaux-Arts/ Émile Lévy, 1910).

ABOVE Louis Claude Vassé (1716–1722), after Edme Bouchardon (1698–1762), *Scale Model of the Equestrian Statue of Louis XV,* patinated bronze, 1759–1763 (Musée du Louvre, Paris).

ABOVE Benoît Louis Prevost (c. 1735–1804/1809), *Equestrian Statue of Louis XV, Place Louis XV*, etching (Châteaux de Versailles et de Trianon, Versailles).
PAGES 42–43 François Denis Née (1732–1817) after Louis Nicolas de Lespinasse (1734–1808), *Perspective View of Place Louis XV in 1778*, print, 1781 (Musée Carnavalet, Paris).

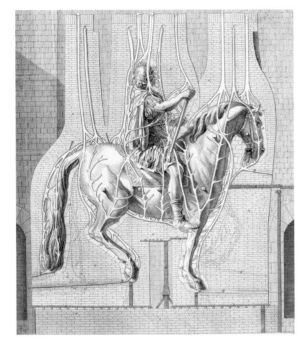 

From the standpoint of the sculptor: Bouchardon produced hundreds of preparatory drawings, detailed anatomical studies of the horse, maquettes in wax, a bozzetto in clay (three years to complete), a plaster model (four years), and, finally, a mold to prepare for the step of the bronze cast (one year). "The casting was done by the lost-wax method before a large, glamorous audience on Saturday May 6, 1758, at four-thirty in the afternoon, taking five minutes and four seconds."[17] It took another five years for the marble-clad pedestal, the two bronze bas-reliefs (paradoxically depicting the king's military conquests on one side and "his love of peace" on the other),[18] as well as the four caryatids at the king's feet (who were allegorical figures of virtues—Strength with her club and oak branch, Peace with her olive branch and cornucopia, Prudence with her mirror ringed by a snake, and, finally, Justice with her scales). Bouchardon, however, died, and was succeeded by Jean-Baptiste Pigalle. The statue was finally installed in unfinished form—only in 1772 did bronze caryatids replace the plaster substitutes present on the day of unveiling.

From the standpoint of the city of Paris: a special workshop was built, as well as a machine to hoist the king onto his pedestal. The city had to borrow "one million [livres] in life annuities in order to pay for the cost of the monument."[19]

From the standpoint of public opinion: Louis was henceforth dubbed "Poorly-Beloved." On the day after the unveiling, a rhyme summed up the general feeling: "Oh the statue so handsome, the base so fine! The virtues walk low, while vice rides high."[20]

On August 11, 1792, when Louis XV had been dead for eighteen years, the Legislative Assembly ordered that statues of kings be pulled down—the colossus of bronze toppled to the ground on the square that would no longer be called Place Louis XV. At that same moment, Louis XVI was locked up in the Temple prison, and five months later he would lose his head on the very spot where the statue of his predecessor came down. Members of the revolutionary Convention who had sentenced the king to death watched from the balcony of the former Royal Wardrobe.

17. Ibid.
18. Ibid.
19. Ibid. It is hard to convert currency of the day, when average household budgets were so different from 2021. But the sum could be said to equal a little less than fifteen million euros today.
20. *Ah! La belle statue, ah! le beau piédestal / Les vertus vont à pied et le vice à cheval.* See Gady, "De la place Louis XV à la Concorde."

45

FACING PAGE Anonymous, *The Equestrian Statue of Louis XV Almost Entirely Set on the Cart,* engraving published in *Description des Travaux Qui Ont Précédé, Accompagné, et Suivi la Fonte en Bronze d'un Seul Jet de la Statue Équestre de Louis XV,* 1758.

ABOVE Pierre Patte (1723–1814), *Cast of the Equestrian Statue of Louis XV in Paris, Unveiled on June 20, 1763* (front and profile), etching (Chalcography Department, Musée du Louvre, Paris).

ABOVE Augustin de Saint-Aubin
(1736–1807), after Hubert François
Gravelot (1699–1773), *The Statue
of Louis XV Unveiled,* print published
in *Description des Travaux de la
Statue Équestre de Louis XV,* 1766
(Musée du Louvre, Paris).

PAGES 48–49 Isidor Stanislas Helman
(1743–1809), after Charles Monnet
(1732–1808), *January 21, 1793.
Louis Capet is Beheaded on Place de
la Révolution,* colored print, 1794.

The Voice of Reason

The king's first choice of a setting for a statue in his honor fell upon the neighborhood around Rue de Buci. But a more reasonable decision finally won out: "Seeing that it was impossible to create a suitable square without destroying merchants' quarters, and without sacrificing the convenience and interests of many of his subjects by demolishing numerous homes …, [His Majesty] has donated to the City a large empty plot of land belonging to him."[21] In fact, that plot was "a kind of marsh where marbles were stored, crossed by several paths leading to open-air cafés, and connected to the Tuileries Gardens by a swing bridge."[22] This solution would have an economic advantage, which in fact prompted it. And it would also have a symbolic impact, since it would create links: on the immediate level, it would connect the Tuileries with the Champs-Élysées—two urban projects developed under Louis XIV—while on a larger level it would create a focal point between the Louvre and Versailles. Yet the idea

BELOW Ole Perrier, after Charles Lesage (1823–1899), *Proposed Position of the Planned Bridge Aligned with Place Louis XV, with its Surroundings,* etching (Bibliothèque historique de la Ville de Paris).

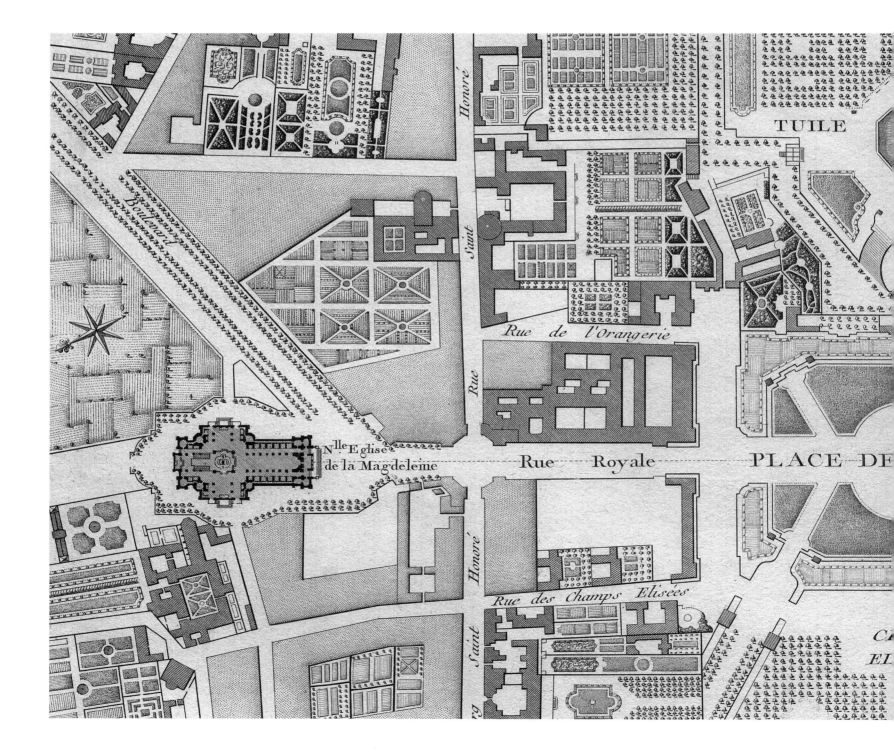

presented one "insurmountable difficulty," in the words of the Marquis de Marigny (who had replaced Tournehem as director of Royal Works): "to create a[n enclosed] square … while simultaneously retaining the magnificence of the fine arrangement of the Tuileries, the esplanade, and the Champs-Élysées."[23]

Most of the original proposals having become obsolete, a second competition was organized, this time restricted to members of the Royal Academy of Architecture. Ange Jacques Gabriel, then first architect to the king and head of the Academy as well as a competitor, was charged with drawing up a synthesis of the various proposals for the new square—creating a kind of concord over the future Place Louis XV. Gabriel came from a long and glamorous line of architects (as was so often the case at the time) dating back to the sixteenth century. The plan he submitted was definitively validated by the king on December 9, 1755, seven years after the original competition was held.

21. Patte, *Monumens érigés,* p. 117.
22. Édouard Fournier, "Promenades dans Paris," *Paris dans sa splendeur* (Paris: Charpentier, 1861).
23. Jörg Garms, ed., *Recueil Marigny: Projets pour la place de la Concorde, 1753* (Paris, Paris Musées, 2002).

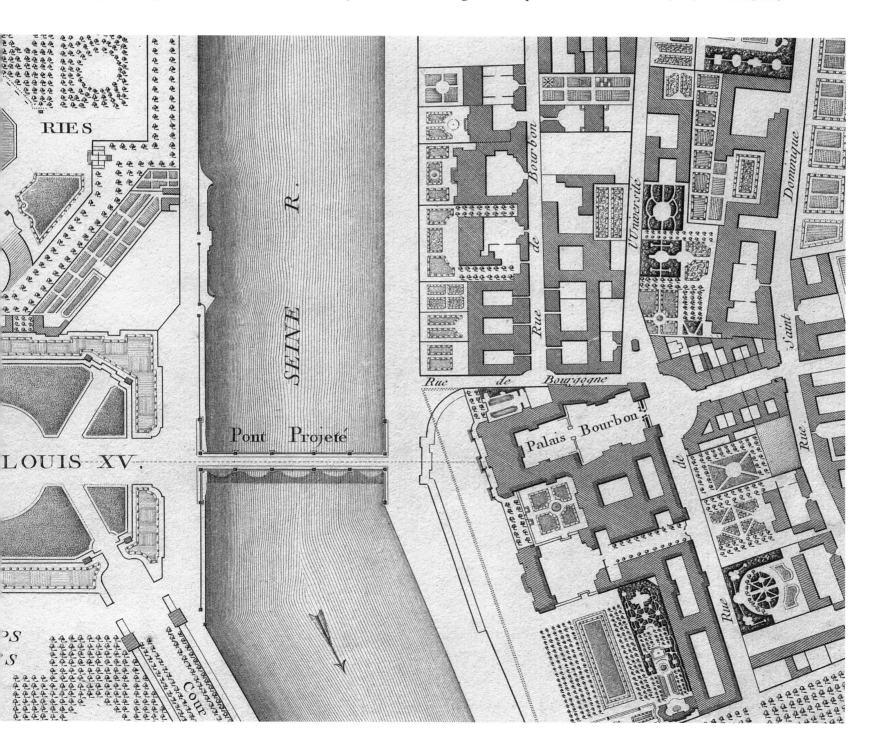

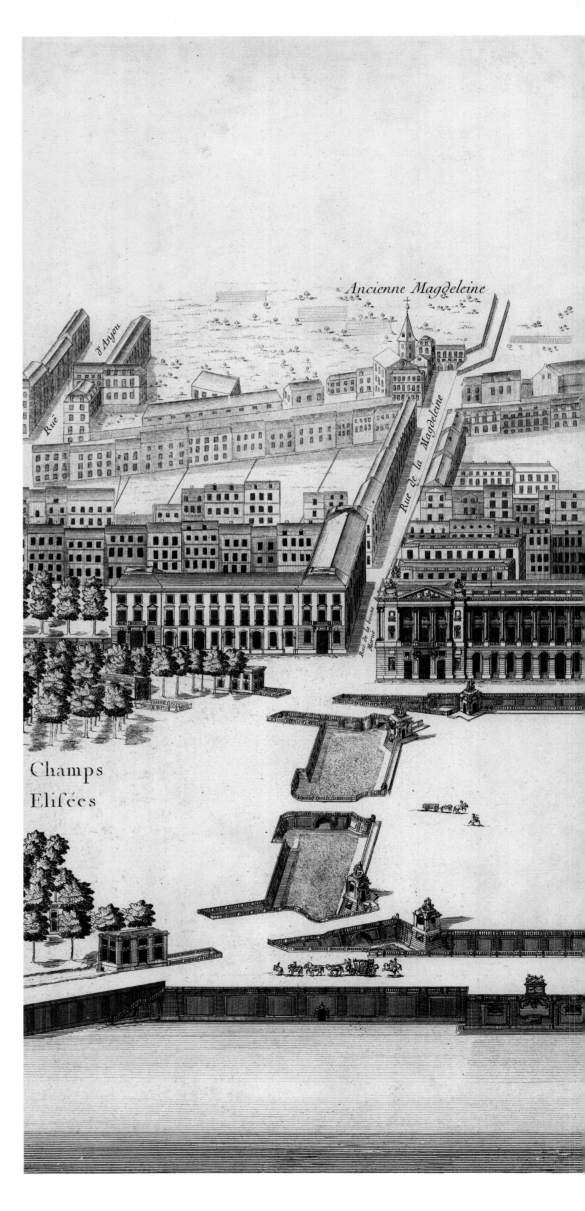

Ancienne Magdeleine

Champs
Elifées

RIGHT Georges Louis Le Rouge
(1712–179?), *Place Louis XV,
Dedicated to the King by His Most
Humble and Most Obedient Servant,
Le Rouge, Geographical Engineer
to His Majesty,* etching,
1763 (Bibliothèque Nationale
de France, Paris).

PLACE DE LOUIS XV.
Dédié au Roi.
Par son très-humble
et très obéissant serviteur Le Rouge,
Ingénieur Géographe de sa Majesté.

Nouvelle Magdeleine

Boulevart

Jardin de la Conception

Assomption

Royale

Ruë St Honoré

Ruë

R. de l'Orangerie

Tuileries

Staging a Masterpiece

On the proscenium was the river; stage left was the Champs-Élysées (fairly wooded at the time); stage right, the Tuileries Gardens and Palace. Upstage, as a backdrop, were two identical buildings, each stretching some one hundred yards. Today's arrangement of the central part of the square, structured like a Roman hippodrome around two fountains and an obelisk from Luxor, gives a poor idea of the original design. Certain sections had stone balustrades flanking ancient-style sunken gardens, over twenty yards wide, reached via steps housed in stone turrets. These ditches—which were filled in during the Second Empire to facilitate traffic—echoed the moats on the Tuileries side, extending that concept to the entire square, forming a cut-cornered rectangle traversed by central paths leading to the statue in the middle. The interplay of different levels, already suggested in several prior submissions for the competition, created an interior zone with a new type of framing—a kind of square in negative, as though the surrounding buildings were sunk into the ground.

This idea was brilliant in more ways than one. First of all, it circumscribed the square while preserving the continuity between the Tuileries and the Champs-Élysées. It thereby overcame the original "insurmountable difficulty." If we momentarily ignore the twin buildings, the architecture of the square played on two opposing yet superimposed levels that generated a witty paradox: a strictly enclosed square, sunk into the ground, completely withdrawn from the city, versus a largely open esplanade thoroughly engaged with its surroundings at eye level.

Another advantage followed from the first: the balustrades and turrets created perspectives that were merely visual propositions which did constrain pedestrians, except, of course, for Rue Royale, enclosed by the two buildings. Symbolic axes radiated from the statue of the king in the middle of the square: one linked it to the divine (the future Church of La Madeleine, then being planned); another looked toward the Louvre and Paris; the one that began at the Champs-Élysées ran all the way to Versailles; and, finally, the southern one led to the Seine, hence to the world. This universal dimension was underscored by two pavilions "for the use of fountain engineers, wardens, and porters,"[24] each on the edge of the two roads fanning westward: Cours de la Reine along the Seine, and another road (never laid out) angling symmetrically toward the plain of Monceau. These two avenues seemed to embrace the sunset, indeed the entire universe, forming a kind of megaphone for the statue of Louis XV, as though the royal voice carried *urbi* in one direction and *orbi* in the other.

Finally, the sunken gardens further contributed to the overall aesthetic impact by creating an architecture of the "void," a poetic space orchestrated like a classical Alexandrine verse with a caesura in the middle, flowing into an open, spectacular panorama that sprawls like free verse, paced by the Seine. To parody Rousseau, it might be said the Place Louis XV was wilder and more romantic than Place Louis Le Grand (now Place Vendôme).[25]

But let us take a loftier look: from exactly seventy-five feet, the height of the twin buildings. Strictly speaking, these buildings are the only elevations on the square—the turreted staircases are closer to what Brigitte de Montclos called architectural "furnishings."[26] The buildings create the veritable vista, both urban and mineral,

24. Patte, *Monumens érigés*, p. 122.
25. "The shores of the Lake of Bienne are wilder and more romantic than those of Lake Geneva." Jean-Jacques Rousseau, *Reveries of the Solitary Walker*, trans. Peter France (London: Penguin, 1979), p. 81.
26. Brigitte de Montclos, in Garms, *Recueil Marigny*.

ABOVE Alexandre Jean Noël
(1752−1834), *Place Louis XV Seen from
the Left Bank* (detail), oil on canvas,
c. 1779 (Musée Carnavalet, Paris).

ABOVE Antoine François Peyre
(1739–1823), *View of the Buildings
on Place Louis XV from One of
the Terraces of the Tuileries* (detail),
watercolor, 1773 (Bibliothèque
Nationale de France, Paris).

since their two façades define the sole line along which the eye must run: up Rue Royale. Yet this line, perpendicular to the axis running from the Tuileries to the Champs-Élysées, remains fairly discreet, limited to the scale of the square itself. What these elevations underscore above all is the straight line they draw, as though extending the direction of the city, parallel to its main avenue. The effect is accentuated by the horizontality of the buildings that, if connected, would be nearly eight times wider than high; and it is further underscored by the design of the façades, which delineate just two levels: the arcaded base combines ground floor and mezzanine (which seems to vanish within the portico) while the colonnade unites the two uppers floors (the attic being hidden behind the balustrade). The central motif of the colonnade imparts rhythm to each building through an uneven number of bays, whose repetitiveness creates an effect of perspective that extends the alignment even further.

Here, then, we have two façades that, together, cover a surface area of fifty thousand square feet and yet seem almost self-effacing in their rejection of monumentality; they exist primarily as a line, an outline, an underline. In this "masterful composition," the twin buildings are merely "precious architectural backdrops" of "airy grace."[27] They are all there is to the square while remaining outside the space it defines, simultaneously observation post and object to be observed.

27. Georges Gromort, *Jacques-Ange Gabriel* (Paris: Vincent Fréal & Cie., 1933).

ABOVE Reinier Vinkeles (1741–1816), *The Royal Garden of the Tuileries Seen from Place Louis XV*, pen and brown ink, watercolor, c. 1770 (Bibliothèque Nationale de France, Paris).
PAGES 58–59 Jacques Philippe Joseph de Saint-Quentin (1738–c. 1785), *Place Louis XV*, oil on canvas, 1775 (Musée des Beaux-Arts et d'Archéologie, Besançon).

Shilly-Shallying

In 1754, when the first stone of the foundations of the statue was laid, the square was still far off.[28] Nothing had begun. Gabriel's synthesis of competing plans had been approved, but in the following year it underwent several modifications. One was of great importance: there had originally been three aligned elevations, establishing two transversal lanes that flanked a main central building. Commentators of the day viewed this a "fundamental flaw" because "no street culminate[d] at the statue, which could not be seen from Rue Saint-Honoré."[29] This was indeed true. But more damaging was the multiplication of ways in to the square, which meant further interruptions in the sunken ditches, completely altering the overall orchestration. It also diminished the horizontality and direction of urban thrust. In that original version, the limits of the buildings were less clear. They extended westward beyond the ditches, turning at a 45-degree angle to block the diagonal axis toward the Hôtel d'Évreux (now the Elysée Palace). Transforming three buildings into two was the stroke of genius that transformed a masterful idea into an absolute masterpiece.

When the statue was unveiled in 1763, the sunken gardens had been dug and laid out, and the façade of the west building rose as high as the colonnade, whereas its eastern twin was only base high. Neither building had been assigned a function.

In 1765, as the first façade was completed, the second had just reached the colonnade. But everything was finally coming together, for the king had decided what would be built behind the façades: the one on the left would house the Mint, while the one on the right would host two other glamorous institutions, the Royal Wardrobe and the Exchequer. Over a two-year period, architect Jacques Denis Antoine worked on the western building while Gabriel worked on the eastern. That was when a double twist occurred: the Mint was ultimately transferred to Quai Conti across the river, allowing the city of Paris to erect a barracks for musketeers behind the western façade, while the Exchequer ceded the entire eastern building to the Royal Wardrobe.

In 1768, as the second elevation was completed, the two façades were supported by temporary structures of wood—a stage set with a still-uncertain role.

In 1772, when the permanent caryatids were finally added to the base of the equestrian statue of the king, the outer construction of the Royal Wardrobe was finished, but not its interior decoration. In the meantime, the city of Paris had renounced its barracks, so the other façade still lacked a building.

In 1774, the Royal Wardrobe moved to Place Louis XV, although the interiors had not yet been completed. The king had died six months earlier, at which point Gabriel retired as royal architect.

In 1775, the building was officially (if not veritably) completed. The city of Paris, still unsure about what to do with the western façade, decided to divide it into lots. Thus three years later, by 1778, four town houses replaced the wooden structure backing the western façade. One, occupied by architect Louis François Trouard, stood behind the pavilion on the left; two others, occupied by financier Daniel Étienne Rouillé de l'Étang and yet another architect, Pierre Louis Moreau, ran behind the colonnade; and a fourth, occupied by Marie Anne de Mailly-Rubempré

28. And the original idea dated back to 1748.
29. Anonymous commentary quoted by de Montclos in Garms, *Recueil Marigny*.

FACING PAGE
The loggia on the southern façade.

(widow of the Marquis de Coislin and a former mistress of the late Louis XV), extended behind the right-hand pavilion. The square had come completely to life, and the Royal Wardrobe opened its doors to the public.

Thirty years had elapsed since the Treaty of Aix-la-Chapelle and the decision to erect a statue celebrating it.

LEFT A perspective view
of the Corinthian capitals
on the colonnade.

RIGHT The restored pediment of
the west pavilion, showing a detail of
Royal Magnificence by Michel-Ange
Slodtz (1705–1764).

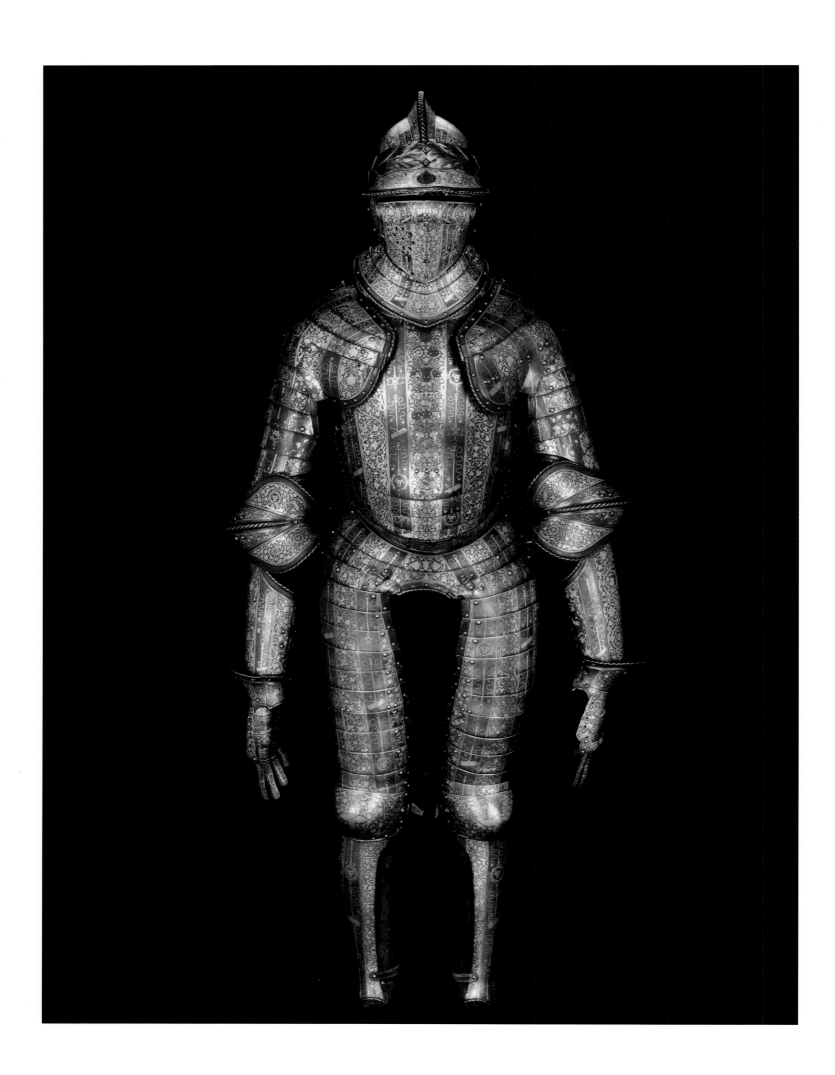

Thus Passes Worldly Glory

The Royal Wardrobe was robbed twice. The well-known incident of the crown jewels was preceded by the more comical theft of royal arms. On July 13, 1789, things began heating up in the streets of revolutionary Paris. Almost all the tax barriers ringing the city had been burned down—people wanted to bring down the price of bread, so eliminating entrance taxes to the city seemed the right kind of pressure. Louis XVI had just dismissed his finance minister, Jacques Necker. A lousy idea: Necker was perhaps the only man people trusted—more or less—and the only one who might have solved the country's financial crisis. The people were hungry, and they needed weapons in order to seize the strongholds where they thought grains were being stored. Did you say weapons? Of course, the king's arms were kept in the Royal Wardrobe! Not that an entire arsenal was housed there. "Only worthy of being kept in the Royal Collection were royal arms and armor, items of beauty, and venerable or highly valued weapons such as those from far-off lands."[30] Which meant Henri II's ceremonial armor (the helmet of which hadn't prevented his death in a tournament), Henri IV's sword, diplomatic gifts from the king of Siam, and medieval shields. Hardly the stuff for storming the Bastille.

But this partial looting of the Royal Wardrobe created one lasting, surreal image immortalized in a drawing by Jean-Louis Prieur: after the theft, the square—not yet rechristened Place de la Révolution—was thronged by "a bizarre battalion wearing a combination of warlike dress from every era and every country both ancient and modern, and bearing all kinds of weapons from Europe, Asia, and America, even the poisoned arrows used by savages. Boucicaut's lance and Du Guesclin's saber were in the hands of a burgher and a laborer, while a porter wielded François I's sword."[31]

The second theft is etched into the building itself—the outline of the cut can still be seen on the shutter that was pierced in order to enter and steal the crown jewels.

It was September 1792. The political situation had greatly changed since the first looting, but the people were still going hungry. For the king, the game was up: three weeks earlier he had been imprisoned in the Temple and elections for a new constitutional Convention had just been held. At the end of the month it would meet for the first time—and would abolish the monarchy. The Tuileries Palace where Louis XVI had resided since his failed attempt to flee the country had been looted and the king's personal staff was massacred (nearly one thousand servants and Swiss guards)—survivors were executed. Prussian troops under the Duke of Brunswick had crossed the border, entering France, as their commander promised, to "inflict an ever memorable vengeance by delivering over the city of Paris to military execution and complete destruction, and the rebels guilty of the said outrages to the punishment that they merit."[32] A wave of panic gripped Paris. It was rumored that imprisoned royalists were fomenting counterrevolution, ready to support the arrival of foreign troops. First the throats of some twenty nonjuring priests were slit as they were being transferred to prison. Then courts were hastily established to order summary executions. In four days, eighty percent of the prison population was slain, including the director of the Royal Wardrobe, Marc Antoine Thierry de Ville-d'Avray. "Following the September massacres, the state of Paris was such that looting with a weapon in hand was an easy, one might almost say everyday, task.

30. Castelluccio, *Le Garde-Meuble*, p. 400.
31. Jean-Louis Prieur, quoted in Jonathan Siksou, "Pillages révolutionnaires," in Gady, *L'Hôtel de la Marine.*
32. The Proclamation of the Duke of Brunswick (known as the Brunswick Manifesto), in J. H. Robinson, ed., *Readings in European History,* vol. 2 (Boston: Ginn, 1906), p. 445.

FACING PAGE The armor of the dauphin, the future King Henri II (Musée de l'Armée, Paris). Made between 1536 and 1547, this ceremonial armor was displayed in the armory room of the Royal Wardrobe, looted on July 13, 1789.

LEFT Pierre Gabriel Berthault
(1737–1831), after Jean-Louis Prieur
(1759–1795), *Looting Weapons from
the Wardrobe on July 13, 1789*,
print, 1802 (Bibliothèque Nationale
de France, Paris).

ABOVE The theft of the crown jewels
from the Royal Wardrobe during
the week of September 11–16, 1792,
print published in Adolphe Thiers,
Histoire de la Révolution Française, 1866.

Brigands, professional thieves, and convicts of all sorts—pickpockets, receivers of stolen goods, cutthroats, and the like—had all been released."[33] It was almost like the introduction to Georges Perec's notorious novel, *A Void*. Without the comedy, but with the letter "e."

Given the highly unusual security situation, the Royal Wardrobe seemed truly vulnerable, especially since it was guarded by a bunch of slackers. Doors were not always locked, and "it often happened that, not being relieved at the right time, men would leave their posts without being replaced," or were so "drunk and intoxicated [that they were] liable to start a fire with their lamps and candles." Sometimes "the guard was comprised solely of children, the oldest being seventeen."[34] And yet never had the display cases and little closed boxes held so many jewels, objets d'art, and unset gemstones, because "the king and queen [had] sent to the Wardrobe all the state jewels they had previously worn during ceremonies."

Since the start of the year, thieves had been casing the Wardrobe on days it was open to the public. Police and court archives point to a certain Paul Miette, soon joined by a "considerable number of individuals organized in gangs with connections between them, who even corresponded with thieves from the provinces." They came from Marseille, Rouen, Brest, and elsewhere, numbering some fifty men in all. During the night of September 11, 1792, some of them acted as lookouts on the square itself (renamed Place de la Révolution less than a month earlier), disguised as police patrols. Others climbed the façade of the building to reach the long gallery of the colonnade, where they cut out a pane of a window, then simply turned the latch, thereby getting straight into the Wardrobe. Over the next three hours, in the flickering light of candles, they lifted several sets of jewelry displayed in showcases, plus "the famous Queen of Pearls (*Reine des perles),* Louis XVI's sword, and two large watches with diamond-studded chains." Then the thieves departed as they had come, ending the night in the shady taverns of Paris.

What? "All that for a few rocks and two tickers?" our crooks might have complained. Not good enough! There was still so much to be had. And therein lay the genius of Miette's plan: ever since the Tuileries Palace had been stormed and the royal family imprisoned, the rooms holding the Wardrobe's treasures were placed under seal. In an ironic twist of fate, while Louis XVI—a great enthusiast of the mechanical arts, who had been caricatured as the locksmith-king—was locked away awaiting trial, fifty thieves recently escaped or released from jail managed the heist of the century thanks to the most rudimentary of security measures. Simple "strips [of cloth] bearing seals that no one dared break due to their legal nature" represented the surest of locks, in legal terms, at any rate. However, the seals barred entry not to the thieves, who had managed to enter the building, but to the guards, halted by the symbolic lock of unbreakable seals on the doors. All the thieves had to do was to proceed stealthily, silently, spreading the job over several nights. It is highly likely that the guards never even passed in front of the sealed doors—even had they made the rounds they would have needed the wits of a master sleuth to figure out the mystery. There was no chance they imagined a robbery was going on.

The night of September 12: no action.

33. Germain Bapst, *Histoire des joyaux de la couronne de France, d'après des documents inédits* (Paris: Hachette, 1889), p. 453.
34. Ibid., p. 458. All subsequent unnoted quotations are drawn from this same source.

75

PAGES 72–73 Pierre Antoine Demachy
(1723–1807), *Unity Celebrations
on Place de la Révolution, 29
Thermidor Year I* (August 10, 1793),
oil on canvas, c. 1793
(Musée Carnavalet, Paris).
LEFT In 1793, symbols of the
monarchy were burned on Place
de la Révolution, in front of the Royal
Wardrobe. In 2017, destruction
occurred within the building, but
this time in an effort to recover the
original ancien-regime magnificence
of the interior. Here the walls, ceiling,
and floor of the former porter's
room have been stripped bare.

The night of September 13: back again. Farewell to the unset gems: the Regent, a one hundred and forty-carat diamond of exceptional purity, considered the most beautiful diamond in the world; the Sancy, a fifty-five carat pear-shaped stone that once graced the fleur-de-lis on Louis XV's crown and was later reset several times at the request of Marie-Antoinette; and thousands of other precious stones.

The night of September 14: rest.

The night of September 15: a binge. After two forays without the least hitch, the thieves were emboldened. "That evening, they made sure to supply themselves with wine and victuals. By the light of the candles they held what must have been a most colorful supper, given the place, the circumstances, and the characters who took part"—allegedly including prostitutes.

On the day of September 16, things began to unravel. Two of the thieves wanted to unload some of their loot: a small box with three diamonds, seven large pearls and several smaller ones—all for six livres. In those days of hardship, six livres would buy a couple of pounds of sugar or a dozen eggs. A police inspector was soon alerted. He found two rubies on the ground where the transaction had occurred, and made the connection with the crown jewels. On arriving at the Wardrobe, he was greeted by the head guard's deputy, who "immediately went to check the seals placed on the doors, and soon returned to assure [the inspector] that the seals were intact. Hence nothing could be missing from the Royal Wardrobe." Duly noted.

The night of September 16: last trick. Employing the same modus operandi, the thieves snapped up everything that remained in the showrooms. "As they came upon an object too big to fit in their pockets, they would throw it to the gallery below, where their colleagues would hurriedly pick it up." It rained gold, silver, objets d'art, historic souvenirs. At the height of the heist, an argument broke out in front of the building between the break-in squad and the lookout team, which wanted its share right away. Drawn by the racket, a patrol of national guardsmen dispersed the troublemakers without really knowing whether they had just prevented a crime or were letting culprits get away with one. Maybe the guardsmen were still debating the point when, all of a sudden, a body fell from the sky and landed heavily at their feet. The man, named Douligny, had broken his leg and had clearly just fallen from the colonnade— any higher, and he would have been dead. A certain Chabert (no known relation to Balzac's Colonel Chabert) was arrested on the top of the street lamp on the corner of Rue de la Révolution (formerly Rue Royale), probably in an effort to reach the treasures of the Wardrobe. And yet, despite this certainty, the guardsmen didn't initially dare to break the seals on the doors; instead, they got long ladders in order to reach the gallery and enter through the window. Miette's ruse had worked far better than anticipated. On the cornice the guards found "a solid-gold vase that the city of Paris presented to Louis XV upon the birth of the Dauphin"; on the terrace there were a gold nef, gemstones, a crown of diamonds and rubies, and the infant's gold rattle with coral handle that Catherine the Great had given to Louis XVI; and the floors of the rooms themselves were "strewn with diamonds. A superb pearl was found in an ivory box, along with a bit-brace, a gimlet, and other items used for breaking in."

Meanwhile, the rest of the team had crossed the Seine, taking the Pont de la Révolution (the bridge formerly named after Louis XVI, now Pont de la Concorde).

Representation

Dans sa vraie grandeur de la Couronne de Pierreries qui a servi au Sacre de.
Louis XV. le 25 d'Octobre 1722.

Renvoy des pierres | de Couleur
4 Rubis | 6 Topases
5 Saphirs | 7 Émeraudes

Completed in 1791, the bridge, which perfected architect Gabriel's inspired vista, now facilitated their escape. Heading down to the banks of the river, they began to divide the loot on this fourth night of theft during which, twice caught by surprise, they littered their path with "many gems, particularly pearls." Each gang went its own way. Some immediately headed for England, others stashed their treasure in disreputable neighborhoods, such as the Allée des Veuves ("Widows' Lane," today known as ritzy Avenue Montaigne).

"On Monday, September 17, at ten o'clock in the morning, when the Assembly had just been called to order, a message [from the ministry of the Interior] suddenly arrived, which a secretary immediately read out: ... The Wardrobe had just been broken into and looted; two thieves had been arrested; police forces had been called; but, he said in conclusion, the jewels had vanished."

Given the value of the crown jewels at the time of the theft, it was certainly the heist of the century. And if we consider their value today, it was perhaps the biggest

ABOVE Antoine Sébastien (1687–after 1761), *Full-Scale Depiction of the Crown of Gems Used at the Coronation of Louis XV on October 25, 1722*, engraving (Bibliothèque Nationale de France, Paris).

ABOVE An upstairs shutter still bears
the scars of the break-in that led
to the theft of the crown jewels in 1792.
FACING PAGE *The Crown Jewels*, lithograph
published in *L'Illustration* no. 2304
(April 23, 1887), (Bibliothèque Nationale
de France, Paris).

burglary of all time. The sixty-nine-carat Bleu de France diamond was valued at three million livres in the 1791 inventory. Drastically re-cut to prevent accusations of theft and harboring stolen goods, today it weighs just forty-five carats—but is reportedly insured for a quarter of a billion dollars!

Thus ends the story of the theft of the crown jewels, which people often view as a founding event in the history of France and the country's collective unconscious. It was a way of turning the page, symbolically, on the monarchy—the price to pay, so to speak, for ushering in a new era. In order to understand what those jewels and their theft still mean today, you merely have to see the crowds in the Louvre's Apollo Gallery, where the meager remains of that extraordinary collection are now on display.

The reality is somewhat different, however. At the conclusion of the police investigation, almost the entire network was arrested. "When comparing the detailed inventory drawn up by the Wardrobe in 1791 with the list of objects recovered after the theft, it turns out that all, or almost all, of the jewels were found, either on the thieves or their receivers, or on private individuals." True, the Bleu de France was not among them. Nor, in general, those that made their way across the English Channel.

On May 20, 1798, the department of the Wardrobe was closed down.

In fact, the crown jewels lived through the revolutionary years for better or worse, and largely for the better. It was the Third Republic, in 1887, that delivered their coup de grâce. "The diamonds, gemstones, and jewels comprising the collection known as the Crown Jewels ... will be sold at public auction. The proceeds from this sale will be converted into government bonds. These bonds will be placed with national banking institutions (*Caisse des Dépôts et Consignations*)."[35] The politician behind that move, Benjamin Raspail, hoped that the bank would thereby finance industrial injuries; Jules Ferry, the minister of fine arts, wanted the income to go to the national museum network. "The sale was held in the Salle des États of the Louvre, in nine auctions from May 12 to 23, 1887. It was a financial disappointment. Placing such a quantity of gems on the market could only lower their value. The historic provenance of the items, so important today commercially, was not taken into consideration."[36] What's more, most leading French jewelers refused to bid, for that would have been committing the treasonous crime of lèse-majesté.

Sic transit gloria mundi.

35. *Journal Officiel*, January 11, 1887.
36. Daniel Alcouffe, "Une catastrophe nationale: la vente des Diamants de la Couronne en 1887," *La Tribune de l'art*, January 23, 2008 (www.latribunedelart.com/une-catastrophe-nationale-la-vente-des-diamants-de-la-couronne-en-1887).

81

ABOVE Michel Berthaud (1845–1912), *Diamonds, Pearls, and Gemstones from the So-Called Crown Jewels*, albumin prints from glass-plate negatives, 1887 (Bibliothèque Nationale de France, Paris).

RIGHT The main reception hall
and the admirals' room prior
to restoration.
PAGES 84–85 Ancient-style masks
on a marble mantelpiece
in one of the reception rooms.
PAGES 86–87 The doors to the naval
chief of staff's formal dining room
prior to their restoration.

A Sense of Place

Photography **AMBROISE TÉZENAS**

Text **GABRIEL BAURET**

The history of photography has impinged on the illustration of French architectural heritage ever since the mid nineteenth century. Their convergence in fact dates back to the famous "Heliographic Mission" of 1851, in which several major photographers were commissioned to compile a visual inventory of emblematic historical monuments all across France. That first, comprehensive public project has served as a regular frame of reference, notably when another remarkable mission was launched by France's national department for regional development (*DATAR*) in the early 1980s. Whereas the latter concerned the French landscape in its totality and diversity, the nineteenth-century mission was governed by the need to record the image of buildings important to French history, whether religious, civilian, or military. The then-new medium of photography—"heliography"—made accurate, detailed pictures possible. At that time, the technology could not yet record interiors; it was first and foremost a question of the buildings' exteriors as seen by the photographers. Establishing a visual record that did not betray reality—hence was objective—would have multiple uses for historians, archaeologists, and posterity.

There have been many ties between photographers and architecture down through history, revealing highly varied approaches and concerns. In the United States, Great Britain, and Germany, as well as France—countries where photographers continued to develop and address new issues—public initiatives existed in conjunction with private ones, collective projects in parallel with individual ones. The technological advances accompanying the history of photography constantly presented new possibilities, allowing photographers to work indoors, in low light, and to discover new viewpoints as well as to extend the dissemination of their pictures. In addition, the concept and culture of "monuments" progressively evolved: it was no longer solely a question of buildings belonging to history, to the past. Photography began documenting the architecture of its own day, and also recorded the industrial revolution that engendered new types of construction embodying progress. During the first half of the twentieth century, a movement like the Bauhaus school made architecture a central feature of its artistic and educational program, thereby bringing photographers and avant-garde designers together. Architectural modernism was accompanied by photographic modernism, as witnessed by the emblematic example of Lucien Hervé, a photographer who faithfully and inventively documented Le Corbusier's architectural output. Yet many other photographers could be mentioned, for the history of photography includes the practice of illustrating architecture, a field that has progressively become an autonomous genre in which documentary record overlaps deliberately artistic exploits.

In the early twentieth century, France established an institution whose goal was to preserve the nation's architectural heritage and to make it accessible to the public. Photography naturally played a role in the mission of that institution, first called the National Office of Historic Monuments and Sites (Caisse Nationale des Monuments Historiques et des Sites) and today known as the Center for National Monuments (Centre des Monuments Nationaux). The institution not only archives and disseminates images of the inventories of these monuments, but also oversees the conservation and restoration of certain buildings from various periods, including recent ones. This is the cultural policy behind the job assigned

PAGE 89 During the renovation.
An interplay of hidden doorways
between Madame Thierry
de Ville-d'Avray's bedroom and
the alcove to Pierre Élisabeth
de Fontanieu's bedroom.
FACING PAGE Prior to renovation.
A hidden doorway under
the Concorde porch.

to Ambroise Tézenas at the Hôtel de la Marine. After having fulfilled several commissions for the Center for National Monuments, Tézenas was chosen to document the site just when work was about to begin on the total transformation of the interior of this majestic building overlooking Place de la Concorde. While the façade remained unchanged—and still perfectly symmetrical with its twin structure to the west—the scope of the work to be done inside, changing the fate of the building, was hard to fathom. Tézenas began taking pictures as early as 2016, one year before work began. The size of the building and the unusual duration of the job had no equal in his previous commissions for the Center for National Monuments at the abbeys of Montajour and Le Thoronet.

While awaiting for the first construction teams to arrive, Tézenas explored every level of the building, from attic to basement, discovering spaces of all kinds—and occasionally losing himself in them. From the walls there seeped a rich, varied, complex past; his eye dwelled on the marks and traces of a history that goes back to the Enlightenment. The Hôtel de la Marine was not spared the disruptions of the French Revolution, but here it seems that the aristocratic gilding did not overly suffer. The building furthermore profited from its symbolic and strategic location when occupied by the German army during World War II. Its history has culminated in the recent departure of the Department of the Navy; the military left behind various furnishings and objects that testify to its presence and activities yet also reflect the protocol associated with the admiralty. Tézenas's initial mission was to record the existing state of things, which meant, according to his own philosophy, "photographing reality without betraying it"—that is to say, without imparting an emotional charge to his images. Tézenas therefore had to find the right balance between taking pictures freely (without, however, turning the site into a field of visual experimentation) and respecting the complete trust shown in him by the Center for National Monuments. His work thus took the form of a lengthy promenade throughout the building, which was also a stroll through history. He makes details speak, yet his pictures also reveal a fine sense of composition. Framing, color, and light are the parameters on which his compositions rest. In the hunt for locations he was guided by his eye, Tézenas being first an observer, only pressing the shutter release later. The use of a tripod enabled him to define the intended shape and outline of the pictures to follow; this approach also dictated the slow tempo of work, while—to pursue the musical metaphor—light determined the key signature. Tézenas "works with" things, but never alters them. Often just a thin ray of daylight illuminates a room. But he also encountered darkness in the belly of the building. The artificial lighting installed by the construction workers who progressively invaded the premises altered the situation, providing the photographer with new visual opportunities. At the same time, his pictures steadily took on color, as light dispelled the mystery.

In the second part of his mission, Tézenas documented the various stages of a terrific transformation over a four-year period. The emptiness of a dormant building, devoid of human presence—a kind of *Flying Dutchman,* to use Tézenas's metaphor of a ghost ship—was replaced by a hectic ballet as the new Hôtel de la Marine neared completion. During his regular visits, Tézenas encountered the various artisans

FACING PAGE View of Madame Thierry de Ville-d'Avray's bedroom in 2016.

carrying out restoration and refurbishment. Spaces slowly filled up with machines, and some rooms even changed shape, completely redesigned. Materials of all kinds participated in the progressive transformation of walls, floors, ceilings, and even roof. The building was covered in scaffolding and tarpaulins; inside, precious items and objects were wrapped up, while murals and mirrors vanished beneath more or less opaque sheets of plastic. Yet they in no way altered the photographer's approach. Tézenas steered the steady course he had set at the start of his mission, even if much of the reality before his eyes no longer looked the same, and might have tempted him down the path of anecdotal details or purely visual motifs.

"Going from a derelict atmosphere to a bustling beehive" is the way Tézenas succinctly describes the transition that took place. The long sequence of his series of pictures conveys the passage from silence to noise, from frozen time to imminent rebirth. During the final months of renovation, everything accelerated and the teams worked feverishly. The eye occasionally dwelled on the gestures of the artisans— woodworkers, painters, and restorers. Rooms where walls and woodwork had acquired the patina of time slowly filled up with furniture and artworks as well as everyday items—a narrative of life in the eighteenth century steadily unfolded, reviving the spirit of the place. But all these events taking place right before the photographer's eyes didn't prompt Tézenas to become a reporter, much less an illustrator. He kept his distance from storytelling. It is only when his pictures are all aligned that a narrative begins to emerge, recounting the architectural, artistic, and historical goals incarnated by the Hôtel de la Marine. The totality of Ambroise Tézenas's work restores the meaning of that tale.

FACING PAGE View of Madame
Thierry de Ville-d'Avray's bedroom
when renovation began in 2016.

PAGES 96–97 Emptied of its furniture, this office was used by the Navy's head of human resources.
LEFT Madame Thierry de Ville-d'Avray's bedroom. The worn wall-linings are being removed. Removing all traces of the Department of the Navy and restoring the eighteenth-century state of the apartment of the intendant-general was the difficult challenge of this experimental renovation, recorded from start to finish by photographer Ambroise Tézenas.

RIGHT Furniture stored
in the corner room.

103

"I had waited eleven long months for these fifteen days that are my only pleasure for the year, and they passed so quickly, so quickly that I now wonder how it is possible that they are over. Is it truly possible that I went to Étretat and spent fifteen days there? It seems I never left the ministry and am still awaiting the vacation … that ended this morning."

Guy de Maupassant, letter to his mother, Paris, September 3, 1875.

FACING PAGE Several writers have worked at the Department of the Navy, including Prosper Mérimée, Eugène Sue, and Guy de Maupassant. The latter was hired in 1872 but resigned in 1878—in 1923 a plaque was put up in his office, room 392.

"She experienced from this tidying the sort of voluptuous pleasure one feels on seeing a void take the place of the objects one has eliminated."

Henri de Montherlant, *The Lepers*

FACING PAGE The former apartment of the intendant-general overlooking a courtyard.

RIGHT A former office, on the third floor overlooking the Rue Saint-Florentin, is completely emptied.

"Silence is the element in which great things fashion themselves together, that at length they may emerge, full-formed and majestic, into the daylight of Life, which they are henceforth to rule."

Maurice Maeterlinck, *The Silence of the Humble*

FACING PAGE The ogival vaults above the loggia.

"The quality that we call beauty … must always grow from
the realities of life, and our ancestors, forced to live
in dark rooms, presently came to discover beauty in shadows,
ultimately to guide shadows toward beauty's ends."

Tanizaki Junichiro, *In Praise of Shadows*

FACING PAGE A door removed
from the disused offices.
PAGES 114–15 The admirals' room
lit by a single LED.

PAGES 116–17 Re-doing the parquet
flooring in the reception rooms.
RIGHT A modern version of
Caillebotte's famous painting,
The Floor Scrapers.

FACING PAGE Protecting the
large chandeliers during work
in the reception rooms.

"We delight in the mere sight of the delicate glow of fading rays clinging to the surface of a dusky wall, there to live out what little life remains to them. We never tire of the sight, for to us this pale glow and these dim shadows far surpass any ornament."

Tanizaki Junichiro, *In Praise of Shadows*

FACING PAGE
Thierry de Ville-d'Avray's
large study.

"Even if a window implies ... a gaze from inward to outward (in this case, from culture toward nature), a door can also be the object of a visual investment, but in the other direction."

Victor I. Stoichita, *L'Instauration du tableau*

FACING PAGE Revealing the original decorative features.

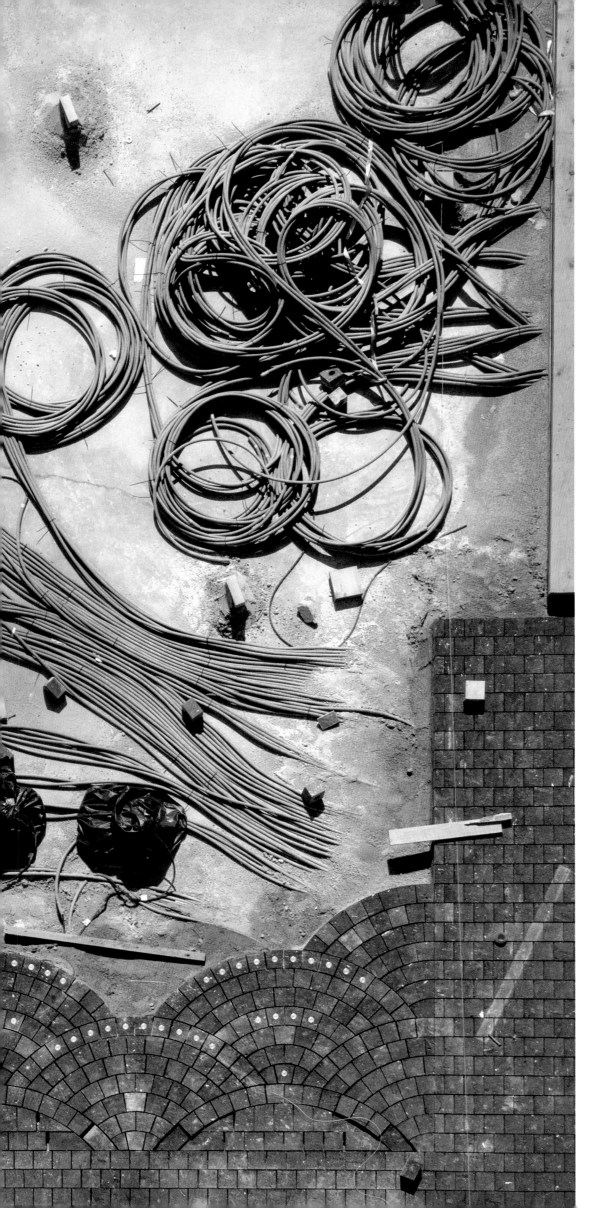

PAGES 126–27 Scaffolding on the loggia.
LEFT The main courtyard being
repaved—LEDs were inserted among
the stones to create a carpet of light.

FACING PAGE The row of rooms in
Thierry de Ville-d'Avray's apartment.
The hallways and service passages,
hidden behind the main rooms, were
included in the overall restoration.

RIGHT The woodwork and original paint
had to be revealed prior to restoration.

LEFT The original decoration in
the mezzanine that held the "flying"
(or elevating) table.

FACING PAGE Stratigraphic probes
and analyses revealed the eighteenth-
century decoration underneath
multiple coats of paint.

"This fatality (no photograph without *something or someone*) involves Photography in the vast disorder of objects—of all the objects in the world: why choose (why photograph) this object, this moment, rather than some other?"

Roland Barthes, *Camera Lucida*

FACING PAGE Eighteenth-century inventories indicated the presence of a wall fountain in the antechamber to the intendant-general's apartment.
PAGE 140 Effects of light on the woodwork.
PAGE 141 Detail of a statue of Hebe in a niche in the antechamber.

"A window opens onto the eternity of a landscape, a door onto the fleetingness of an act of love or daily routine."

Georges Banu, *La Porte au cœur de l'intime*

FACING PAGE **The doors to the dining room after restoration.**

FACING PAGE The silk lampas being applied to the walls of Thierry de Ville-d'Avray's bedroom.

"I put a picture up on a wall.
 Then I forget there is a wall.
 I no longer know what there is behind this wall,
 I no longer know there is a wall,
 I no longer know this wall is a wall,
 I no longer know what a wall is."

Georges Perec, *Species of Spaces*

FACING PAGE Paintings hung on the silk-lined
walls of Thierry de Ville-d'Avray's bedroom.
PAGE 148 A chased, gilt-bronze wall clock.
PAGE 149 The alcove bed being installed in
Thierry de Ville-d'Avray's bedroom.

LEFT The painted glass in the mirror
room was protected by plastic sheeting
during the work.

"Doors suit in an interior perceived as a whole.
From within this quiet, private, inner space, you watch for
visitors who halt at the threshold. Doors favor a communion
between the visible interior and the outer eye that explores it.
The beholder looks in from the outside, implicitly entering
an interior that offers no resistance and thus encourages
a voyage to the most profound recesses of the self."

Georges Banu, *La Porte au cœur de l'intime*

FACING PAGE In the antechamber to the large study,
a hidden door rests against the paneled wall.

155

LEFT Some five hundred doors were restored, requiring as many handles.

156

RIGHT Lock box, strike plate,
and handle on the door to Thierry
de Ville-d'Avray's large study.

LEFT Madame Thierry de Ville-d'Avray's
bedroom being refurnished.

FACING PAGE Pictures in Madame
Thierry de Ville-d'Avray's bedroom,
hung to align with the bed.
PAGE 162 The hallway leading to Thierry
de Ville-d'Avray's antechamber and large study.
PAGE 163 The service passage to Thierry
de Ville-d'Avray's large study.

"The frame separates the image from everything that is non-image. It defines everything within the frame as a signifying world, whereas the world outside the frame is simply experienced. We may wonder, however, which of those two worlds the frame belongs to."

Victor I. Stoichita, *L'Instauration du tableau*

FACING PAGE Painted silks and woodwork in Thierry de Ville-d'Avray's large study.

FACING PAGE An eighteenth-century
ceremonial sword on a writing desk, a loan
from the Musée des Arts Décoratifs, Paris.

FACING PAGE A dressing table in the bathroom
of Thierry de Ville-d'Avray's apartment.
PAGE 170 The row of rooms leading from
Thierry de Ville-d'Avray's bedroom
to his bathroom.
PAGE 171 The window in Madame Thierry
de Ville-d'Avray's bedroom overlooking
Place de la Concorde, the Orangerie,
and the Tuileries Gardens.

"I wonder if my readers know the color of that 'darkness seen by candlelight.' It was different in quality from darkness on the road at night. It was a repletion, a pregnancy of tiny particles like fine ashes, each particle as luminous as a rainbow."

Tanizaki Junichiro, *In Praise of Shadows*

FACING PAGE Throughout the intendant-general's apartment there is a quest for the flickering, incandescent effect of candlelight.

Periods of Time

JÉRÔME HANOVER

A Grateful Nation

It's the guys from the Navy who saved the Royal Wardrobe. Starting in 1789, when Louis XVI was forced by revolutionary events to leave Versailles and return to Paris, various royal ministries also moved to the capital. The Navy people were first consigned to a small part of the pavilion on Rue Royale but steadily took over the entire building. By 1796 it was all theirs: the Office of the Royal Wardrobe became the Department of the Navy (or Hôtel de la Marine). The sailors stayed until 2015.

When studies first began for the major renovation described here, it slowly became clear that nearly eighty percent of the original features of the private apartment of the intendant-general of the Royal Wardrobe were still present, in addition to the interiors preserved in the stately rooms used by the naval ministry. Stratigraphic probes showed that beneath successive layers of paint, the one from the 1770s had survived. Almost nine windows out of ten were over two hundred and fifty years old. It thus became clear that the very heart of the former Royal Wardrobe still offered a unique record of eighteenth-century decorative arts. Not just any old record, but testimony to the royal lifestyle led by the intendant-general of the Wardrobe, rivaling the quality of Versailles. Its excellence and magnificence can be detected not just in the perfect alignment of the stonework on the façade but also in the splendor and lavishness of the interior decoration and furnishings. The king's "showroom" was very much like the king's own home. Or maybe even better, insofar as the first intendant-general to move in, Pierre Élisabeth de Fontanieu, had a "flying" (or elevating) table installed, that is to say one equipped with a mechanism that lowered it to the floor below, where servants could set and clear it without ever entering the dining room. Not even Versailles had the like. Louis XV had considered installing an elevating table at the Trianon but abandoned the idea.

PAGE 175 For the first time in France, the systematic removal of successive layers of paint was extended to entire interiors.
FACING PAGE Like the façade on Place de la Concorde, the main courtyard of the Hôtel de la Marine was built of pale Saint-Leu limestone.
ABOVE The clock in the main courtyard.

If today no other government building offers such a good picture of royal lifestyle during the ancien régime, the reason is primarily political. It was easy for the revolutionaries to appoint one of their own to head the ministries and departments in charge of trade, justice and policing, all professions in which certain commoners had become wealthy, creating a bourgeoisie. But when it came to the armed forces, things were more complicated. Getting into the military academy wasn't as simple as enrolling in a law school, so none of the revolutionaries had the right skills. Plenty of them were courageous enough, of course, but cannon fodder won't suffice to win a war. Trained and experienced strategists are also required. The aristocrats had been doing it for centuries, whereas the commoners had been trying their hand at revolution for a mere matter of months. A gradual transition was required—all the more so once most of Europe entered into a coalition against France; even certain provinces, lead by La Vendée, were resisting the Parisians' revolutionary aspirations. All the officers working in the former premises of the Wardrobe thus came from the royal armed forces. They may or may not have been amenable to revolution, but in any event they weren't the type of people to smash up interiors. On the contrary, they were more likely to discourage the looting of a building strongly reminiscent of the ancien régime.

And later, once things had settled down a little, a cultural attitude safeguarded the premises. Who, better than sailors, knows the importance of keeping things shipshape? The Greek word *tekton,* from which "architect" is derived, could mean both carpenter and shipbuilder. Indeed, large boats are equipped with "cabins" and a luxury ship is dubbed a "floating palace." Sailors at sea take good care of their ship—and the same was true of the landlocked Royal Wardrobe. As with a hull in dry dock, they regularly repainted the walls of the Hôtel de la Marine for over two centuries, coat after coat, never removing the layer underneath, which had the virtue of preserving the very first coat.

ABOVE A perspective view of the loggia.
FACING PAGE Lit by large windows giving onto the courtyard, the main staircase features a wrought-iron and bronze banister designed by ironsmith Claude Roche.

Unfortunately, the exceptional condition of these eighteenth-century interiors does not apply to the whole building. Even at the time, not everywhere had been decorated, such as the storerooms and workshops. Major changes had also been made in the nineteenth century (the galleries were altered and their decorations taken down, while two upper floors were gradually added and fitted out with rooms). In fact, in the mid twentieth century a concrete building almost replaced the one designed by Ange Jacques Gabriel—it would have been inserted behind the surviving façade. Fortunately, that never happened.

The impeccable work of Christophe Bottineau, the executive architect at the Historic Monuments Commission who oversaw the renovation, underscores the perfection of the building, and just how criminal it would have been to destroy the interior. "The original layout is extremely clear, always just right. Every staircase is intelligently located with respect to the building's function, adhering to a policy of double circulation, vertical and horizontal. Gabriel was nearing the end of his career, and had achieved such mastery of his art that he optimized the architectural impact through an extraordinary economy of means. When a plan is so pure and powerful, the premises can only be reoccupied by sticking close, with great tact, to the original policy."[37]

As different as its current role and function are, the new Hôtel de la Marine has thereby recovered its nearly authentic layout, so that its two successive states do not merely enter into a dialogue across the ages but even "simultaneously touch, like giants immersed in Time, across widely separated years and the distant periods they have lived through."[38] Partition walls have come down; original volumes are once again at home. The former warehouses, called "magazines," have become stores and restaurants, while the upper floors house offices. The same approach has been adopted throughout: alter as little as possible. The new roles, by reconnecting with original functions, make the intelligence of Gabriel's plan and layout all the more apparent. The heart of the plan was to open the building to the public, as Louis XV wished. The military, however, keeps its mouth shut by tradition, so the Navy long imposed silence on the building. But now the Royal Wardrobe has given it the floor again. The building is again part of the city, open to it on Place de la Concorde and Rue Royale, weaving its own zones of circulation into the urban fabric—the main courtyard has become a quiet, covered square behind the grandiose esplanade. The courtyard brings a new landmark and breath of fresh air to the neighborhood, acting like a transitional space between outside and inside, namely the exhibition spaces being opened for the first time since 1792, restoring the museum-like role incumbent on the Wardrobe when it originally moved in. The former furniture galleries, which became the Navy's ceremonial reception rooms, will host temporary exhibitions and provide access to the loggia behind the colonnade. Some of the treasures in the Al Thani Collection will be displayed in the Tapestry Gallery. The intendant-general's apartment, a rare surviving example of eighteenth-century French lifestyle, can now be seen as it was in the days when Intendant-General de Fontanieu, followed by Intendant-General Marc Antoine Thierry de Ville-d'Avray and his wife, received their guests, with all the accuracy of a faithful reconstruction as well as all the spirit and presence typical of inhabited dwellings.

37. Interview with Christophe Bottineau, March 22, 2021.
38. An allusion to Proust's *Time Regained*.

FACING PAGE The staircase leads to the grand dining room, formerly the armory room of the Royal Wardrobe. The doors, decorated with trophies featuring quivers and flaming torches, were restored to their eighteenth-century state.

182

RIGHT The antechamber displays
neoclassical simplicity with an
antique-style niche and statue
harmonizing with the white-glazed
stove. The piles of books on the table
evoke the Enlightenment atmosphere
and the scholarly interests of
Intendant-General Pierre Élisabeth
de Fontanieu.

PAGE 184 The hallway leading to
Thierry de Ville-d'Avray's large study.
The further you progress into the
private rooms, the more magnificent
they become.

PAGE 185 A sofa made by Georges Jacob
(1738–1814) sits below a still life
by Claude-François Desportes
(1695–1774), *Game, Fruit, Cat and
Parrot* (on loan from the Louvre).

RIGHT The large study of the new
intendant-general, Thierry
de Ville-d'Avray, who installed his
private rooms in the space where
his predecessor, Fontanieu,
had set up two scientific labs.

PAGES 188–89 AND ABOVE The panels
of painted silk on the walls of the
large study feature neoclassical
grotesque motifs.
FACING PAGE Tieback and tassel on
a curtain in the large study.

Resurrection

In the intendant-general's apartment, Time has not dishonored History; nor History, Time. Delphine Christophe, conservation director at the Center for National Monuments, says there survived "all the architectural clues permitting an accurate reconstruction that showed the public what an inhabited eighteenth-century apartment looked like."[39] That approach is experimental from a museum standpoint because elsewhere in the world there is a tendency to display masterpieces of decorative art as showcase items taken out of context and stripped of their human function, whereas their very essence is to express a way of life, to play their part in an overall composition. The historical approach taken to the intendant-general's apartment is entirely different: while scholarly and unimpeachably authentic, it seeks first to resurrect the premises, to incarnate both a building *and* a period, "occupying a place in Time infinitely more important than the restricted one reserved for them in space."[40]

"Restoring an historic monument is not hard science—it calls above all for a sensibility. The Royal Wardrobe project brought together players whose points of view converged: a main contractor [the Center for National Monuments], a project manager [Christophe Bottineau], and interior decorators. Joseph Achkar and Michel Charrière contributed all the artistry that would have been lacking in this restoration had the approach been purely scholarly."[41] Admittedly—conservators conserve and decorators decorate. In a museum, liveliness is often on the side of the beholder; to make life present on both sides, which encourages dialogue, and to recreate the sensibility of a place designed to be lived in required skills other than the usual ones. The two interior decorators, Achkar and Charrière, worked on an exhibition site for the first time,

39. Interview with Delphine Christophe, March 23, 2021.
40. An allusion to *Time Regained*.
41. Interview with Delphine Christophe, March 23, 2021.

192

ABOVE Detail of the mantelpiece in the large study. It is made of Portoro marble decorated with chased, gilt-bronze mounts by Pierre Philippe Thomire (1751–1843).
FACING PAGE Full view of the fireplace in Thierry de Ville-d'Avray's large study. On the mantel is a clock decorated with children playing musical instruments, plus two painted porcelain vases (on loan from the Manufacture Nationale de Sèvres).

PAGE 194 The parquet flooring in the large study.
PAGE 195 The writing desk with filing cabinet in the large study.

after thirty-five years of restoring and refurbishing private residences, that is to say, real living areas. The difference is significant: "Museums play an educational role, but in order to recreate a sense of the eighteenth century—especially among young people—it had to be brought back to life. We had to show that the decorative arts, even the most lavish masterpieces, are first of all items used every day, and therein lies their charm and poetry. You have to get them out of the spotlight, desanctify them. That's crucial today in order to arouse curiosity and appreciation for the poetic side of this place."[42]

Whereas, in France, renovating tends to mean redoing (repainting, regilding, revarnishing, reweaving, reframing, reflooring), the resurrected feel of the intendant-general's apartment springs from the opposite approach: one by one, square inch by square inch, layers of paint were removed with a scalpel. On certain walls there were up to sixteen coats. In some areas, tiny reconstructions were required. The same techniques, the same meticulousness, and the same sense of heritage employed on an old master painting were applied to this apartment of eight thousand square feet. Just revealing the stairwell called for twenty-five of these surgical painters. Having largely survived, the underlying decoration thus resurfaced. Behind the naval chief of staff's stainless-steel kitchen was the intendant's gilded study, found almost intact, with its original cornice, wood paneling, and fireplace; and beneath the tile floor was the original parquet.

That is how, little by little, the intendant-general's apartment reclaimed the premises, as though he had never left them. Is that a restoration? No, Your Majesty, it's a resurrection.

42. Interview with Michel Charrière, February 23, 2021.

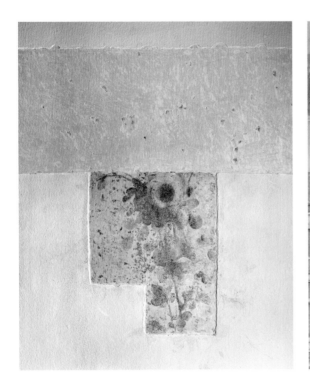

FACING PAGE Detail of woodwork and wallpaper in the physics cabinet, or lab.
ABOVE, LEFT Uncovering eighteenth-century floral decoration in a small room on the mezzanine level.
ABOVE, RIGHT Excavating the paintwork to reach the oldest layers of paint.

The Vast Edifice of Memory

Two intendant-generals, one after another, lived in the private apartment of the Royal Wardrobe over a twenty-year period. That's a blink of an eye by the architectural clock, or little more than a knowing wink by the building's own lifetime. But by narrative standards, it's an eternity. Which story or stories should be told when many of them contradict one another? There's the story of the bachelor intendant-general, de Fontanieu, who fitted out a "room of mirrors" that was decoratively painted not just with floral friezes and cherubs but also with naked vestal virgins who probably vied with the intendant-general's young female guests. Then there was Intendant-General Ville-d'Avray, whose wife insisted that painters modestly veil those same breasts, which she had no wish to contemplate. The two intendant-generals embodied two different periods, two reigns, two sociological backgrounds—hence two different tastes.

The Fontanieu family had held the office of intendant-general for three generations. Grandfather Moïse Augustin had purchased it under Louis XIV, consecrating a social rise that lifted the Fontanieus from the world of finance in the late seventeenth century. The family's nobility was probably not as old and glamorous as the heirs would claim, and the Duke of Saint-Simon, in his *Memoirs,* could scoff at that former "lackey of [wealthy banker] Crozat who became, after due payment, keeper of the Royal Wardrobe."[43] Moïse Augustin nevertheless had good taste, integrity, and a certain administrative talent, for he drew up the earliest surviving inventories of the Wardrobe. His son and heir, Gaspard Moïse, was an intellectual, having attended the prestigious Louis-le-Grand school; his library included "numerous manuscripts and approximately ten thousand printed volumes covering many fields."[44]

43. Quoted in Stéphane Castelluccio, *Le Garde-Meuble de la Couronne et ses intendants, du XVIᵉ au XVIIIᵉ siècle* (Paris: Éditions du Comité des Travaux Historiques et Scientifiques, 2004), p. 22.
44. Ibid., p. 28.

PAGES 198-99 The small study in Thierry de Ville-d'Avray's apartment overlooks a courtyard.
ABOVE Two views of the "room of mirrors," delicately painted with mildly erotic scenes. Putti gambol among garlands of flowers and exotic birds, whereas the originally nude female figures were modestly draped at the request of Madame Thierry de Ville-d'Avray.

FACING PAGE With its reclining sofa and suggestive atmosphere, this private boudoir wonderfully evokes the rakish bachelor, Intendant-General Fontanieu.

ABOVE Chinoiserie-themed wallpaper
in the powder room. As everywhere
in the restored apartment, the light
fixtures recreate a candlelit atmosphere.
FACING PAGE The hallway leading
to the powder room.

He even wrote some of them himself, and translated others from Italian. Gaspard was able, "through his cultivation, sensibility, and very good knowledge of the artistic milieu, to chose the best artists and craftsmen," thereby acquiring works by Antoine Robert Gaudreaus and Jean-François Oeben for the royal collection.[45] When Pierre Élisabeth inherited the office upon the death of his father, architect Gabriel was designing the building for the Wardrobe. The vulgar world of finance was far in the family's past—the Fontanieus had become marquesses, had traveled, had read, had written, and were said to be "witty and cultivated."[46] Over three generations they handed down their experience of the office, their working methods, and their intellectual rigor, curiosity, and passion for the arts and its techniques. The superintendency of the Royal Wardrobe was in their blood. Pierre Élisabeth was an aesthete, artist, and scientist. He set up two physics and chemistry "cabinets," or labs, where he created synthetic stones from crystals and oxides. He published technical treatises. He was an enlightened amateur, one of those many intellectuals shaped by the Enlightenment. Pierre Élisabeth maintained "direct, sometimes personal and friendly, relations with artists and craftsmen."[47] Might he be described as more bohemian than his father? Probably not—but he was certainly an epicure, and would have been considered a dandy in a later era.

The last of the Fontanieus was the first intendant-general to move into the Royal Wardrobe. He monitored all the work and chose all the decoration, "conceiving the apartment in its totality."[48] He was fully aware of the political importance of Louis XV's plan and made sure that the premises conveyed not just the power of king and kingdom but also a sense of taste and lifestyle with which both men sought to influence the entire world.

Whereas the Fontanieus left a profound mark on the history of the decorative arts, the Thierrys are another story. A story that began, a century and a half before their arrival at the Wardrobe, in the kitchens of Louis XIV, where four generations of the family worked hard serving the king—from esquire of the table to chef, and from chef to groom of the bedchamber—until finally ennobled. There were far from rich, were not great readers, and were not known for their passions—except perhaps for Christ. But they had patience and determination. Marc Antoine Thierry had perhaps more than the others; after "fairly successful studies, at age fifteen he was admitted into the Gray Musketeers,"[49] rising from sergeant to captain of dragoons, then lieutenant colonel and *mestre de camp* (colonel) before taking up his father's office of groom of the bedchamber and thereby winning the trust of Louis XVI. His wealth grew—by a lot. He bought a small property with its associated seigniorial rights in Ville-d'Avray, near Versailles. In 1783 Marc Antoine obtained unexpectedly, given his pedigree, the reversion of the office of intendant-general of the Wardrobe, a post he assumed the following year upon the death of Fontanieu. Shortly after, Louis XIV elevated Ville-d'Avray to the status of barony. Marc Antoine "rapidly became an embodiment of 'favorite' in the most negative sense of the term—a parasite who deceives, exploits, and misuses royal generosity."[50] We must nevertheless recognize his education, which his forebears lacked—he showed a mild interest in literature, the natural sciences, and, vaguely, history. He also reorganized his administration, making it more efficient at a time when royal commissions were on the increase as several châteaus were being refurnished.

45. Ibid., p. 30.
46. Ibid., p. 48.
47. Ibid., p. 49.
48. Interview with Joseph Achkar, February 16, 2021.
49. Quoted in Castelluccio, *Le Garde-Meuble de la Couronne*, p. 64.
50. Ibid., p. 79.

FACING PAGE The physics cabinet, whose instruments evoke Fontanieu's interest in science and his penchant for making imitation gemstones.

RIGHT Pierre Élisabeth de Fontanieu's gilded study. The eighteenth-century woodwork and decoration were discovered intact behind the stainless-steel walls of a kitchen installed here in the twentieth century. One of the two fireplaces had been moved to the former library, while the other went to the Navy's command center. They were returned to the study, whose walls have been relined with red damask from that period.

When Marc Antoine Thierry de Ville-d'Avray moved into the Wardrobe, then, "everything was already there: interior decoration, fabrics, tapestries, and so on. But he wanted to leave his mark on the place. What affectation to seek to impose his own taste there where Fontanieu had been!"[51] The picture room became his wife's bedroom; the green brocatelle lining the walls was replaced by lampas woven in three colors. In the gilded study, an imitation fireplace was added opposite the existing one; the chemistry cabinet became an audience room; and a lavish bathroom was added. Successive inventories indicate "increasingly dense furnishings"[52]—Ville-d'Avray's changes tended toward the excessive and ostentatious. And were sometimes historically nonsensical: "according to the inventories, in the corner room there had been a set of tapestries illustrating the Life of Esther, which [Ville-d'Avray] replaced with Louis-XIV-period tapestries that didn't correspond to the setting. They weren't the right dimensions, so panels and strips had to be added."[53]

This apartment is thus really two apartments—not placed on top of one another, but intermingled in a single interior. There is no Fontanieu layer beneath the Ville-d'Avray layer (unlike the eighteenth-century coat of paint beneath the later layers applied by the Navy). Some rooms are the product of one man or the other, but most display their double influence. Sometimes three periods coexist harmoniously: in his bedroom, Fontanieu installed exceptional wood paneling from the 1750s, taken from the Hôtel de Conti, to decorate half of that 1770s-style room. He later had the paneling reproduced to cover the other half when he removed the red damask lining the walls while creating an antechamber.

The intendant-general's apartment has had its day. It was impossible to return it to an allegedly original state, for which there exist—at best—just brief descriptions, whereas outstanding if slightly later features have survived. Given the gaps, it was hard to choose between the Ville-d'Avray option, which would have reinforced the coherence of the last-known state, or the Fontanieu option, often more subtle and harmonious. And what was to be done with the coffered ceiling installed in the audience room in the nineteenth century? "An inventory is just a snapshot. We can see from the archives, by examining orders and deliveries, that change was constant. The work was done during a transitional period. So a reconstruction would have been a betrayal."[54] Indeed, we need to imagine the effervescent atmosphere of the Wardrobe—the constant ballet of deliveries and removals, the vast, rolled-up tapestries being hoisted up the staircases, the artisans working on restorations, the bustling administrative staff, and so on. You can't bring a dynamic history back to life by immobilizing it, postcard-like. March 2, 1775 (the day work was officially completed); May 30, 1784 (the day Fontanieu died); August 15, 1792 (the day Ville-d'Avray was arrested); or May 20, 1798 (the day the Office of the Wardrobe was shut down): even had a scholarly reconstruction of any one of those key dates been possible, none would have conveyed the spirit of either the building or this restoration project.

The scene played out in the intendant-general's apartment today is not set some time between those four dates, but shows the dynamics that interconnect them. The eighteenth century comes back to life through a whole series of snapshots—exposures that, "though momentary, are sufficient to compose a complete tableau vivant and, as it were, an historical scene."[55]

51. Interview with Joseph Achkar, February 16, 2021.
52. Interview with Delphine Christophe, March 23, 2021.
53. Interview with Joseph Achkar, February 16, 2021.
54. Interview with Delphine Christophe, March 23, 2021.
55. An allusion to Proust's *Cities of the Plain*.

FACING PAGE The corner room, overlooking Rue de Rivoli and the Tuileries to the east, and Place de la Concorde to the south, has recovered its original magnificence. Two Gobelins tapestries from the *New Indies* series designed by Claude François Desportes, *The Camel* and *Two Oxen*, add a rich touch of exoticism to the lavish interior (on loan from the Mobilier National).

PAGE 210 The fireplace in the corner room. The musical clock with automatons was among the masterpieces that were tracked down in order to reconstruct Thierry de Ville-d'Avray's apartment—it was delivered to the intendant-general around 1784.

PAGE 211 A detail of the Griotte marble mantelpiece adorned with gilt-bronze rams' heads and vine branches.

When the Absent Speak

"The tone is set right from the intendant-general's staircase."[56] The banister is original; molding added in the nineteenth and twentieth centuries has been removed; the sconces have been reinstalled. The trompe-l'oeil painting of dressed stone on the walls has resurfaced. Beneath that painting, the real stone has fissured, hence has been touched up in some places while in other places the damage has been retained as a mark—a stigma—of passing time. In order to bring the apartment back to life, it has to look as though it has truly lived.

The aligned row of rooms, in accordance with classical French interiors, follow an order from plainest to most magnificent. "People didn't flaunt their wealth in the vestibule, where there wouldn't be any gilding or parquet flooring; the walls would be lined with plain fabrics like cotton or linen."[57] This reflected a social code, "a way of honoring guests based on where they were received."[58] A tradesman would wait in the armory room whereas a peer would be welcomed to the corner room. In the latter half of the eighteenth century, this class symbolism also resonated with Enlightenment philosophy, for the increase in majesty from simplest to most lavish was also a dialectic leading toward the greatest privacy and intimacy—at the end of the route was Madame Thierry de Ville-d'Avray's bedroom.

The first antechamber of the intendant-general's apartment has a stone floor, and two paintings recently purchased in Italy now replace ones no longer there. They correspond to the description in the inventory—scenes of ancient stones. Countering this mineral coldness, the fabrics of the slightly offset curtains suggest that something might be going on behind them. It is like a call for witnesses. Not a reconstruction, but rather a reminiscence—this is not an historically accurate stage set, but a historical setting with theatrical appeal. Every time a visitor moves through this succession of spaces, he or she has the impression of entering a room that history has just exited.

A little further on, Madame Thierry de Ville-d'Avray has just returned to the apartment. A dress laid over a chair waits for her to change. "It is not a court gown, but a dress of printed fabric as worn at home in the eighteenth century," just like the ones she might have put on every day.[59] A charming object in the midst of masterpieces, it adds a poetic touch and enlivens the scene.

56. Interview with Joseph Achkar, January 18, 2021.
57. Interview with Joseph Achkar, March 2, 2021.
58. Interview with Christophe Bottineau, March 5, 2021.
59. Interview with Michel Charrière, March 2, 2021.

FACING PAGE The staircase leading to the intendant-general's private apartment.
PAGE 214 The statue of Hebe in the niche in the antechamber dates from 1760.
PAGE 215 Also in the antechamber, a detail from a capriccio—or imaginary view—of ancient architecture inspired by Bolognese artist Il Mirandolese (Pietro Paltronieri, 1673–1741).

LEFT The gaming table in the corner
room is left as though the game
has just been interrupted.

218

RIGHT Madame Thierry de Ville-
d'Avray's bedroom in dusky light.
PAGE 220 A portrait of a woman
as Diana can be seen between the
drapes of the Polish-style canopy.
PAGE 221 The top of the canopy.

FACING PAGE Aligned with Rue de Rivoli,
Madame Thierry de Ville-d'Avray's
bedroom faces due south,
overlooking Place de la Concorde.
ABOVE The lavish tassels for
the curtain ties were made by the
Declercq furnishings workshop.

RIGHT Madame Thierry de Ville-d'Avray's bedroom was installed in 1786–87 in Fontanieu's former picture room. With walls lined in green brocatelle, this room reflects the refinement of eighteenth-century decorative interiors.

FACING PAGE The fireplace of blue
Turquin marble in Madame Thierry
de Ville-d'Avray's bedroom.
ABOVE, LEFT A small bedside table
with everyday accessories—a Sèvres
porcelain cup, an embroidered
purse, and a fan.
ABOVE, RIGHT A detail of the green
brocatelle wall fabric and a bell pull.
PAGES 228–29 Detail from the frieze
of gilt-bronze medallions on
the fireplace in Madame Thierry
de Ville-d'Avray's bedroom.

"At the time, people of a certain station had no glass on the table where they ate. Bottles, decanters, and glasses sat on a side table until a diner asked to drink. At which point a servant brought those things over, poured a drink, and then took everything back to the side table once the diner had drunk—a practice that even applied to the king."

Roland Jousselin, *Au couvert du roi*

FACING PAGE A door opening onto the dining room, offering a glimpse of a space that has come "alive," reflecting the savoir-faire of the period.

RIGHT The dining room in Marc Antoine Thierry de Ville-d'Avray's apartment. The reconstructed table setting is based on a painting by Jean François De Troy (1679–1752), *Dining on Oysters* (Musée Condé, Chantilly).

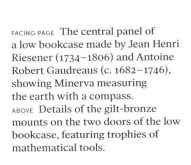

FACING PAGE The central panel of
a low bookcase made by Jean Henri
Riesener (1734–1806) and Antoine
Robert Gaudreaus (c. 1682–1746),
showing Minerva measuring
the earth with a compass.
ABOVE Details of the gilt-bronze
mounts on the two doors of the low
bookcase, featuring trophies of
mathematical tools.

FACING PAGE AND PAGES 238–39 The painted silk fabric lining the walls of the dining room was reconstructed from inventory descriptions and from designs by ornamental painter Alexis Peyrotte (1699–1769). Very similar to the original, the pattern of ribbons with flowers and exotic birds, plus medallions of rural scenes, is designed to give the impression of a marvelous garden.

ABOVE The table is set with mythological figurines and porcelain bottle-coolers.

240

ABOVE AND FACING PAGE The fabric
is gros de Tour, a type of silk taffeta,
heated with an iron to give it
a patina of age.

And in that moment a memory unfolds, "just as the Japanese amuse themselves by filling a porcelain bowl with water and steeping in it little crumbs of paper which until then are without character or form, but, the moment they become wet, stretch themselves and bend, take on color and distinctive shape, become flowers or houses or people, permanent and recognizable."[60] People were here a moment ago, in the dining room. A guest has left his vest on the back of a chair. In eighteenth-century France, tables were not set; it wasn't until the following century that "Russian-style service" (aligning cutlery, plates, and glasses at each guest's place) became part of the French lifestyle. In the days when the intendants-general of the Wardrobe hosted dinners, everyone arrived with a servant who filled glasses and plates (the very job at which the Thierry family began its social climb) and brought them to the table from a side room housing a large marble cooler. Perhaps Fontanieu has just left the room with his guests, leading them to his physics cabinet to show them his latest invention. Or maybe he is taking young, flirtatious ladies to his "room of mirrors". Whatever the case, the table is exhibited as though the meal is over, as seen in a painting of a similar table by Jean François De Troy, *Dining on Oysters* (Condé Museum, Chantilly). In that painting, "each detail is a still life in itself: the onion stalks, the overturned glasses, the discarded napkins. On the floor are oyster shells, straw, wine-coolers, and ice. The painting is so successful due to a casualness in the realism of the scene. People are having fun. Eighteenth-century society liked to party. It was frivolous."[61] All that energy is evoked here simply, from the thick-glassed bottles of champagne to the magnificent plates of silver, from the Sèvres porcelain to the rustic baskets. Here, time has come to a halt; the apartment itself is recalling something: it probably witnessed such a scene.

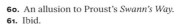

60. An allusion to Proust's *Swann's Way*.
61. Ibid.

242

ABOVE A side table in the dining room.
FACING PAGE An eighteenth-century French coat "casually" draped over a chair in the dining room.

The Weave of Time

Textiles were long the most precious goods in the Royal Wardrobe. Richly embroidered, woven with gold thread, they were enlivened by rigorously regular patterns or painted with scenes that rivaled the ones done on canvas or panel.

The "flying shuttle," designed to accelerate weaving, arrived in France in 1747 along with its English inventor, John Kay. Forty years later, the first steam-driven looms would trigger the industrial revolution. In 1801, an industrialist from Lyon, Joseph Marie Jacquard, invented the loom that now bears his name. Suddenly a single worker could produce brocades and complex damask patterns—like the ones lining the walls of the intendant-general's apartment—that previously required an entire team of weavers. The second half of the eighteenth century set the stage for a technological revolution that would transform the status of fabrics in the following century. Less costly, fabrics thereby became less precious. But in the days of the Royal Wardrobe their lavish presence still indicated the host's affluence.

Textiles are fragile. They are easily damaged and inevitably deteriorate. As with the paint on the walls, any clash with eighteenth-century interior decoration, furnishings, and objects would have created a temporal cleft, a kind of glaring hiatus that might have skewed the entire historic approach. Such a blunder would have engendered disbelief. "The scale of values couldn't be reversed."[62] Hence there are miles and miles of fabric in the intendant-general's apartment, covering walls, windows, alcoves, fire screens, door, beds, cushions, etc. And they are all coordinated, of course. It took years for Achkar and Charrière, the two interior decorators, to come up with enough yards of period material to upholster almost all the chairs. When it came to the walls, things were sometimes complicated. Finding an identical pattern in such quantity was a true challenge. But it was met, with a crimson damask, in the gilded study.

62. Interview with Delphine Christophe, March 23, 2021.

FACING PAGE The sumptuous curtain fabric in Madame Thierry de Ville-d'Avray's bedroom.
ABOVE, LEFT Fabrics placed on the mantelpiece in the corner room.
ABOVE, RIGHT A detail of the red damask and a bell pull.

246

ABOVE The wear on this floral
fabric was accentuated to lend
it greater authenticity.
FACING PAGE The green brocatelle in
Madame Thierry de Ville-d'Avray's
bedroom was rewoven by the
Tassinari & Chatel firm based on
eighteenth-century archives.
It combines the sheen of silk with
the rusticity of jute in order to match
weaving techniques of the period.

The panels were assembled
by hand, without perfectly aligning
the pattern.
PAGE 248 The alcove and bed in the
bedroom on the courtyard side were
upholstered in crimson damask.
PAGE 249 Detail of the fabrics
in the alcove in Thierry de Ville-
d'Avray's bedroom.

In Madame Thierry Ville-d'Avray's bedroom, an inventory from the Fontanieu period listed a green brocatelle, long vanished. "We had to recreate the effect of thread colored with a vegetable dye. It took over twenty attempts to get the color right."[63] For the blacksmith-themed lampas in the intendant's own bedroom, "a highly faded eighteenth-century swatch, so deteriorated it was almost invisible, was used as a model for an extremely pale weave to which a blue vegetable dye was added to recreate the accuracy of the fabric."[64] In the dining room, from which three painted panels had vanished, a "reconstruction based on descriptions"[65] evokes the atmosphere of dinners at the Royal Wardrobe. That entailed a gros de Tours—or coarse-weave silk taffeta—in which latticed ribbons, foliage, flowers, and birds are orchestrated around central medallions depicting classical-style landscapes. The medallions were originally painted by Alexis Peyrotte, some of whose works survive in Fontainebleau and as far abroad as Sweden, providing the patterns now rewoven in modern fabric. The overdoor panels, painted with birds, are the originals, and even though they were done by a different artist they were conceived jointly. "There was a theme, a coordination—things didn't go off in all directions."[66] However, in a room where the paintings are two hundred and fifty years old, "it had to look as though the fabric had aged with the walls."[67] So a hot iron was used on the gros de Tours. Everywhere "the darning of worn patches was done by hand, using vegetable pigments, because the subtlety of colors has disappeared from chemical dyes. All the modern fabrics were repainted and given a patina."[68] This means that the intendant-general's dining room today has curtains, chairs, and panels all imbued with the same poetic atmosphere, imparting great realism to the scene.

63. Interview with Michel Charrière, March 2, 2021.
64. Ibid.
65. Ibid.
66. Interview with Joseph Achkar, March 2, 2021.
67. Interview with Michel Charrière, March 2, 2021.
68. Interview with Michel Charrière, February 23, 2021.

ABOVE AND FACING PAGE The silk lampas upholstering the bed and alcove in Thierry de Ville-d'Avray's bedroom required elaborate research into the color and wear of the fabric.

LEFT Thierry de Ville-d'Avray's bedroom.

RIGHT A personal touch in Thierry
de Ville-d'Avray's bedroom.

257

LEFT The bedroom overlooking
the courtyard, along with the "room
of mirrors" and the gilded study, are
reconstructions of the apartment
in the days of Pierre Élisabeth
de Fontanieu.
PAGE 258 Tieback and tassels
on the curtains.
PAGE 259 Bedroom with rococo
paneling that Fontanieu transferred
from the Hôtel de Conti, where
the Royal Wardrobe had been
temporarily housed.

FACING PAGE Detail of the rococo
woodwork in the bedroom
overlooking the courtyard.
ABOVE An overdoor in
the corner room.

Furniture Regained

The furniture in the intendant-general's official apartment—like the walls, decorations, fabrics, and candelabra—belonged to the king. Some of it is still owned by the National Furniture Depository (*Mobilier National*), the democratic successor to the Royal Wardrobe. There it sat patiently in conservation storerooms or in the nation's stately homes. Some of it went to other museums, but much was sold, for example Thierry de Ville-d'Avray's bedroom furniture, bought by an American who had it upholstered in nineteenth-century fabrics and then donated it all to the Museum of Fine Arts in Boston. Everything, however, was described in inventories, item by item.

"Right from the start of the project, it was decided to buy an equivalent piece if it proved impossible to recover the original furniture. Sometimes that meant an even better piece, since the alcove bed replacing the one in Ville-d'Avray's bedroom is probably of higher quality—it's attributed to Georges Jacob."[69] In general, however, the pieces listed in the inventories have found their way back home. In those inventories, they were described in a straightforward manner. The gilded study, for example, had a "veneered wood writing cabinet richly adorned with fire-gilt bronze mounts and white marble top crowned by a gallery" and a "flat-topped desk of the same wood, very rich, adorned with bronzes like the writing cabinet." The dimensions of each are given. Those simple descriptions identified two major pieces of French decorative art, ordered by intendant-general de Fontanieu from Jean Henri Riesener before the latter became cabinetmaker to the king. The "flat-topped desk" is none other than the Muses desk, "one of the most charming examples of French cabinetmaking …, the finest piece of marquetry ever produced by Riesener …, a matchless piece of furniture."[70] On its top are two allegories of Geometry and Astronomy, while "scrolling foliage sprouts from a corner fleuron then curls back

[69] Interview with Joseph Achkar, March 2, 2021.
[70] Alfred de Champeaux, *Le Meuble* (Paris: A. Quantin, 1885), pp. 225 ff.

THE FRENCH ROYAL WARDROBE

ABOVE AND PAGES 264–65 Detail of the top of the Muses desk, decorated with allegorical figures of Geometry and Astronomy. The Muses desk has returned to its home in the gilded study. This exceptional piece of furniture, with a hidden mechanism, was ordered by Fontanieu in 1771 from cabinetmaker Jean Henri Riesener (on loan from the Louvre).
FACING PAGE The writing cabinet in Thierry de Ville-d'Avray's apartment.

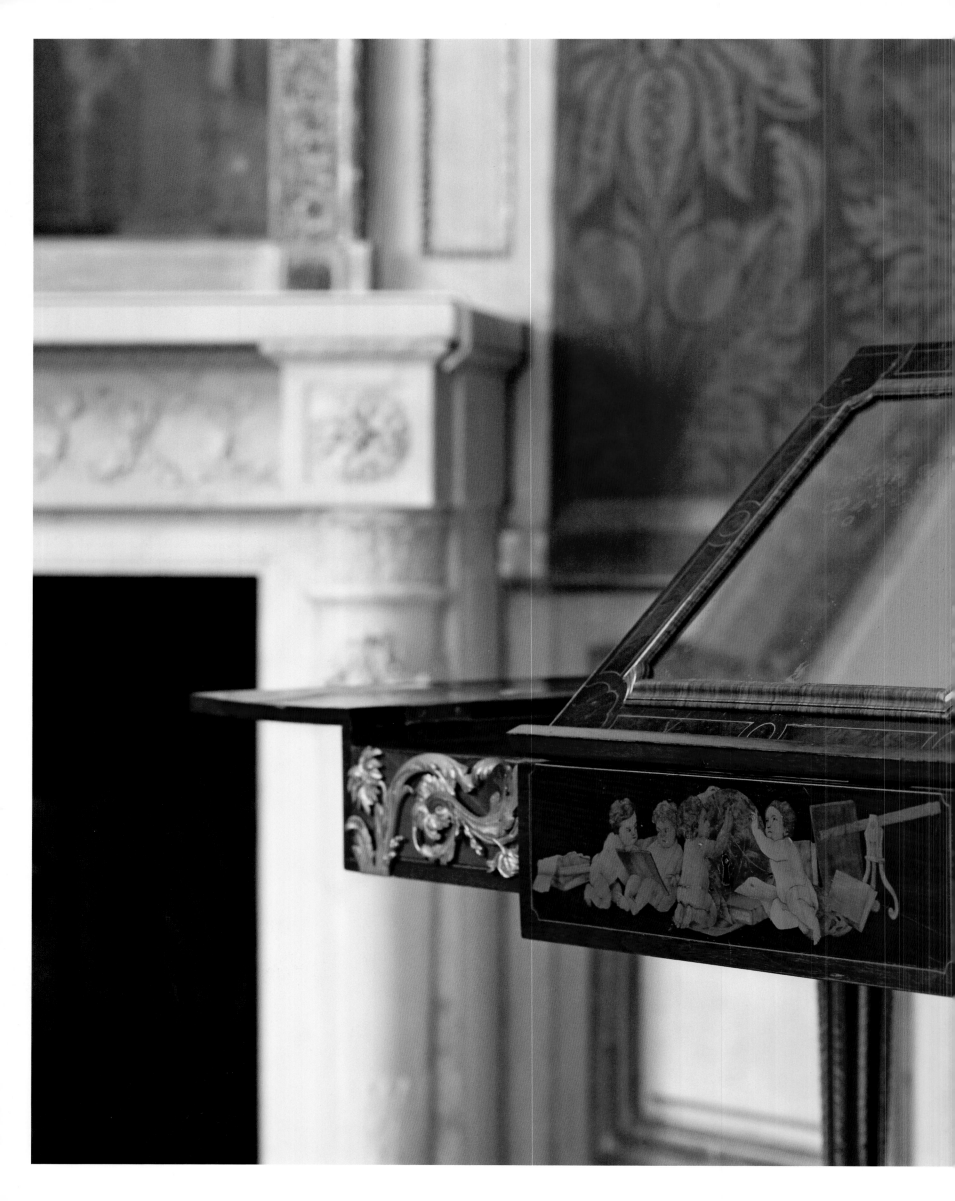

ABOVE AND FACING PAGE Details of the
"writing cabinet" in the gilded study.
Part of the order of 1771, the piece,
with its sumptuous marquetry, stood
against a wall and served as a writing
table. It came up for auction in 2018,
and was thus reacquired, becoming
the only one of its kind by Riesener
in a French public collection.

with peerless grace."[71] A secret mechanism opened the front, like a drawer, to create a reading stand. Formerly in the Petit Trianon, the desk has now been returned to the intendant-general's gilded study, generously loaned by the Château of Versailles. It thus joins the writing cabinet that stood opposite it in 1771, which was bought at auction by the Center for National Monuments. The intendant-general's apartment is graced by other dispersed wonders by Riesener—a sideboard formerly in the Élysée Palace has been moved to the dining room; a commode donated by the Al Thani Foundation has settled into Madame Thierry de Ville-d'Avray's bedroom. "No lapse of taste can be found in any of [Reisener's] furniture, whose carefully studied lines are enhanced by marquetry of great refinement and bronzes of perfect grace. He was endowed with true creative genius."[72]

In Thierry de Ville-d'Avray's audience room is a desk made by Antoine Robert Gaudreaus (on loan from the Department of the Army), upon which sit candlesticks, a seal, an inkwell, various accessories, and the Royal Wardrobe portfolio, as though the intendant-general had just received a visitor. On a pier table is a liqueur service. "It is the sum of many details that create the spirit and poetry of a place,"[73] for they desanctify the masterpiece on which they sit: "they make a ceremonial setting more human, they snuff out the pretentiousness."[74]

For the first time since the end of that period, the eighteenth century seems both alive and livable in this museum where "history takes priority over objects."[75]

71. Ibid., p. 226.
72. Ibid., p. 214.
73. Interview with Michel Charrière, March 2, 2021.
74. Interview with Joseph Achkar, March 2, 2021.
75. Ibid.

FACING PAGE This commode by Riesener, dated 1774–75, placed in Madame Thierry de Ville-d'Avray's bedroom, was donated by the Al Thani Collection Foundation.
ABOVE Details of the gilt-bronze mounts on the commode by Riesener.

PAGES 270–71 AND LEFT The library
and study next to Madame Thierry
de Ville-d'Avray's bedroom.

274

RIGHT The bathroom in Thierry
de Ville-d'Avray's apartment.

Face to Face

"In the nineteenth century, the height of the building was raised for purely functional reasons, destroying its proportions."[76] That's not visible from the square, of course, for the façade was listed as an historic monument in 1862, but the additional floors in the back distorted Gabriel's architecture and drastically reduced the sun reaching the courtyards. (The entire building was not listed until 1977.) Given real estate pressures, no one would think of eliminating the ungainly addition now, especially since the loan taken out by the Royal Wardrobe to finance the restoration work will be reimbursed thanks to income from renting the office spaces partly located in the two additional floors.

It is not hard to imagine that the Wardrobe, where they know how to resuscitate the past, could make buildings disappear. Which is what happened: a pyramidal glass roof was set on the eighteenth-century cornice, masking the upper part of the building, thereby restoring the original proportions. The polished stainless-steel structure streaks across the sky over the courtyard, crisscrossing more or less densely in a projective drawing that, in its pure geometric abstraction, recalls a flock of geese in flight. This twenty-first-century glass roof was designed by Hugh Dutton in collaboration with executive architect Christophe Bottineau of the Historic Monuments Commission. But employing a visual effect to bring the image of the courtyard closer to the original one was not sufficient to fully respect the overall ethic: its basic conception also had to resonate with an eighteenth-century attitude.

Enclosing the courtyard, creating a covered area where the museum's pathways can be organized, established a kind of link between the periods. That is not merely its function, but its very nature. "Only by grasping the way eighteenth-century chandeliers worked did this particular roof emerge. It imitates the idea of catching and reflecting light—the mirrors, gilding, the multiple flickers of candles, the faceted crystals, and so on. In the intendant-general's courtyard, that same logic was deployed in a modern idiom, perfectly calculated thanks to simulation software that came up with the ideal proportions."[77] Thus after a century and a half of dimness, the light that had drenched the intendant-general's apartment prior to the additions was restored, via reflection.

76. Interview with Christophe Bottineau, March 22, 2021.
77. Ibid.

FACING PAGE AND PAGES 278-79
View of the intendant-general's courtyard with the new glass roof designed by Hugh Dutton and Christophe Bottineau to amplify luminous reflections.

By Way of Conclusion

"Certain people, whose minds are prone to mystery, like to believe that objects retain something of the eyes which have looked at them, that old buildings and pictures appear to us not as they originally were but beneath a perceptible veil woven for them over the centuries by the love and contemplation of millions of admirers," wrote Marcel Proust.[78] Are we twenty-first-century folk prone to that mystery, we who like nothing better than referring to the spirit of this and the spirit of that, while often misrepresenting the true history, nature, and function of many objects? Behind that veil, the eighteenth century seems blurred—not by the time that has elapsed, but by the distance created by sanctification. Too often, museums imprison everyday life in display cases, turning ordinary items into curios. Museums freeze life like a painting, offering a somewhat bourgeois picture of a period—which would probably raise Pierre Élisabeth de Fontanieu's hackles, because it distorts the spirit of eighteenth-century France. No one would be shocked—not even the most chauvinistic French historians—by the statement that "Italy and the Renaissance trampled over medieval France even though its buildings, fabrics, furnishings, silverware, and illuminations displayed a refinement superior to anything found elsewhere in the world."[79] For nearly two centuries, nothing seemed able to resist the cultural hegemony of Rome and its heirs. France recruited Italian painters, sculptors, architects, and musicians. French artists, meanwhile, trained in Italy. Did the so-called "major" arts have to remain an Italian privilege? The return of French cultural influence only began in the second half of the seventeenth century, then increased during the following one. "People began to consider the decorative arts as a major art. The bronze mounts on furniture steadily became veritable sculptures of great subtlety and refinement, whereas Italian furniture was made to be taken in at a glance."[80] Maybe therein lies the spirit of the eighteenth century, in its determination to elevate everyday items and surroundings into a lifestyle, a savoir-faire. And France's Royal Wardrobe might well be the most eloquent and most spectacular example of its achievements. By raising the curtain on their staging of the intendant-general's apartment, Joseph Achkar and Michel Charrière have lifted the "perceptible veil" mentioned by Proust in *Remembrance of Things Past*. The eighteenth century suddenly seems nearer, more real. It illumines the French spirit, a spirit that is not merely a style. It is expressed not just in the artistry of Riesener's Muses desk, but in the very choice of an everyday item as a medium of expression. The Muses desk could not convey that idea if placed on a pedestal, under a spotlight. It had to recover its true place—in Fontanieu's gilded study, one of the smallest rooms in the apartment as well as one of the most private. It had to engage with the room's gilding, damask-lined walls, and Versailles-parquet floor. As magisterial as the desk is, it had to be just one of the highlights along the way: part of an arrangement, a restoration, a way of life that is itself, on the whole, a work of art. "The greatness of true art … [is] to rediscover, to reapprehend, to make ourselves fully aware of that reality, remote from our daily preoccupations."[81]

78. An allusion to *Time Regained*.
79. Interview with Michel Charrière, March 2, 2021.
80. Ibid.
81. An allusion to *Time Regained*.

FACING PAGE
In the recption rooms, the doors and the fireplace are reflected in mirrors set in the woodwork.

LEFT Beyond the reception rooms
is a diplomatic office that contains
the desk on which the French decree
abolishing slavery was signed on
April 27, 1848, by Victor Schoelcher,
the Under-Secretary of State
for the Navy and Colonial Affairs.
PAGE 284 The admirals' room
after restoration.
PAGE 285 The diplomatic office.
This is where the crown jewels
were kept in the days of the
Royal Wardrobe.

Selected Bibliography

ALCOUFFE, Daniel. "Une catastrophe nationale: la vente des Diamants de la Couronne en 1887," *La Tribune de l'art*, January 23, 2008 (www.latribunedelart.com/une-catastrophe-nationale-la-vente-des-diamants-de-la-couronne-en-1887).

BAPST, Germain. *Histoire des joyaux de la couronne de France, d'après des documents inédits*. Paris: Hachette, 1889.

CASTELLUCCIO, Stéphane. *Le Garde-Meuble de la Couronne et ses intendants, du XVIe au XVIIIe siècle*. Paris: Éditions du Comité des Travaux Historiques et Scientifiques, 2004.

FOURNIER, Édouard. "Promenades dans Paris." In *Paris dans sa splendeur*. Paris: Charpentier, 1861.

GADY, Alexandre. *L'Hôtel de la Marine*. Paris: Nicolas Chaudun, 2011.

GARMS, Jörg. *Recueil Marigny: Projets pour la place de la Concorde, 1753*. Paris: Paris Musées, 2002.

GROMORT, Georges. *Jacques-Ange Gabriel*. Paris: Vincent Fréal & Cie., 1933.

MOREL, Bernard. *The French Crown Jewels*. Anvers: Fonds Mercator, 1988.

PATTE, Pierre. *Monumens érigés en France à la gloire de Louis XV*. Paris: Chez l'Auteur, Desaint et Saillant, 1765.

ROSERTO, Alphonse. *Edme Bouchardon*. Paris: Librarie Central des Beaux-Arts/Émile Lévy, 1910.

Sources of Quotations

BANU, Georges. *La Porte au cœur de l'intime*. Paris: Éditions Arléa, 2015.

BARTHES, Roland. *Camera Lucida*. Translated by Richard Howard. New York: Hill & Wang, 1987.

DE MAUPASSANT, Guy. *Correspondance*. Vol. 1. Évreux : Le Cercle du Bibliophile, 1973.

DE MONTHERLANT, Henri. *The Lepers*. Vol. 2 of *The Girls*. Translated by Terence Kilmartin. London: Weidenfeld & Nicolson, 1968.

JOUSSELIN, Roland. *Au couvert du roi*. Paris: Éditions Christian, 1998.

MAETERLINCK, Maurice. *The Silence of the Humble*. Translated by Alfred Sutro. New York: Dodd, Mead & Co., 1903.

PEREC, Georges. *Species of Spaces*. Translated by John Sturrock. London: Penguin, 2008.

STOICHITA, Victor I. *L'Instauration du tableau*. Paris: Méridiens Klincksieck, 1993.

TANIZAKI, Junichirō. *In Praise of Shadows*. Translated by Thomas Harper and Edward Seidensticker. London: Vintage, 2001.

Index of Names

Page numbers in italic refer to captions.

Acknowledgments

Éditions Flammarion wishes to thank the Centre des Monuments Nationaux for entrusting it with the conception and creation of this book. The publisher is particularly grateful to Philippe Bélaval, Antoine Gründ, Jocelyn Bouraly, Edward de Lumley, Laurent Bergeot, Anne Lesage, Blanche Legendre, Christophe Bottineau, and the teams supporting them. Its thanks also go to Ambroise Tézenas, whose discerning eye has immortalized four years of work on the project; Joseph Achkar and Michel Charrière for their care and support; Jérôme Hanover for his inquisitive and scholarly foray into the history of the Royal Wardrobe and the rebirth of the Hôtel de la Marine; and Gabriel Bauret for his sensitive interpretations of the photographic images.

The Centre des Monuments Nationaux thanks its sponsors for their support in the restoration and reopening of the Hôtel de la Marine:
Al Thani Collection Foundation, Joseph Achkar and Michel Charrière, Velux Foundation, Siaci Saint Honoré, Ponant Foundation, Rolex Foundation, and JCB card, as well as Monsieur and Madame James and Jacky Lambert, Madame Danièle Ricard, and Monsieur Gérard Descours.

The Centre des Monuments Nationaux also wishes to express its appreciation to the financial supporters who have made it possible to restore the Hôtel de la Marine to its historical splendor:
Al Thani Collection Foundation; Banque de France; Centre National des arts Plastiques; Château de Parentignat; Château, Musée et Domaine National de Versailles; Fondation des Artistes; Ministère des Armées; Mobilier National; Musée Carnavalet – Histoire de Paris, Crypte Archéologique; Musée de la Chartreuse de Douai; Musée des Arts Décoratifs; Musée des Beaux-Arts de Chambéry; Musée des Beaux-Arts de Marseille; Musée du Louvre, Département des Peintures, Département des Objets d'Art; Musée National de la Marine; Musée National des Arts et Métiers; Musée National et Domaine du Château de Pau; Sèvres – Manufacture et Musée Nationaux; Sotheby's France; as well as Messieurs Joseph Achkar and Michel Charrière; Madame Gilberte Beaux, Monsieur François Hayem, Monsieur Anne-François de Lastic, Monsieur Bruno Thierry de Ville d'Avray, Monsieur Jacques Thierry de Ville d'Avray, and Monsieur Marc Thierry de Ville d'Avray.

For his constant support and great care throughout the project in guiding Ambroise Tézenas through the labyrinth of the Hôtel de la Marine, the Images Department of the Centre des Monuments Nationaux and the editorial design team wish to express their warmest gratitude to Yann Kerjean.

Gabriel Bauret is very grateful to Anne Lesage for her hospitality and helpfulness, and to his wife, Chantal Bauret, for her unflagging support during his work.

Jérôme Hanover thanks Joseph Achkar, Laurent Bergeot, Christophe Bottineau, Michel Charrière, Delphine Christophe, Deke Dusinberre, Karine Huguenaud, Bernard Lagacé, Lara Lo Calzo, Christophe Parant, and Suzanne Tise-Isoré.

Ambroise Tézenas expresses his heartfelt thanks to Laurent Bergeot, Yann Kerjean, Blanche Legendre, and Anne Lesage.